The Story of **BODIE**

The Story of BODIE

BY

ELLA M. CAIN

With Introduction by

DONALD I. SEGERSTROM

FEARON PUBLISHERS
2450 Fillmore Street
San Francisco 15, California

In cooperation with
DONALD I. SEGERSTROM
MOTHER LODE PRESS
Sonora, California

Foreword

During the Western expansion of these United States hardy and industrious Americans and Europeans were slowly developing the farming and timber lands on the outposts of civilization. It took the impetus of the discovery of gold in California and Nevada to cause a stampede westward such as the world has never known. Towns born of these discoveries sprang up over night, and, in a few months, housed a population of five, ten, and even fifteen thousand struggling humans.

Many of these towns are now deserted "ghost towns" and practically uninhabited, but they have left a heritage to these United States in a phase of American life that is well worth chronicling.

Such names as Hangtown, Marrietta, Calamity Jane, Julia Bulette and Jessie James are recognized by those who know the West, because much has been written about them, but Joseph DeRoche, Charlie Jardine, Pioche Kelly, and the rich lodes of Bodie, California, are practically unknown. Their stories have not been recorded in print, although the number of those who were shot, hanged, or run out of Bodie defy enumeration.

By 1869 the river of gold-seeking humanity had whirlpooled onto the eastern highlands of the Sierra Nevadas, into the Paiute country of Mono Basin, until the pinnacle was finally reached on "the top of the world in Shooter's Town."

"The Bad Man from Bodie" was a slogan that flashed

around the United States in the early 70's. It originated from the fact that the vigilantes, who called themselves the "Citizens Committee of 601," took the law into their hands to suppress and control the lawless element of the camp. Scores of bad characters were given 24 hours to leave town—or else. Therefore, many an upright citizen, hailing from this distant camp, was embarrassed by the greeting "Are you the bad man from Bodie?"

As far back as I can remember I had a feeling that sometime I would write the story of Bodie, my birthplace, and my home town. This much I can tell you in truth: This history is authentic. These stories are true. These characters are real people, who made up the colorful background of this old camp. This history, these people, have been part of my life.

My father, M. J. Cody, came to Bodie in 1879, having, under President Cleveland, received an appointment as Land Office Receiver for this part of the West. In 1881 he married Catherine Shaughnessy of Virginia City, Nevada. I was born in Bodie in 1882. Several years later my father was elected Sheriff of Mono County, and the family moved to the County Seat in Bridgeport.

My childhood was spent there and later I was sent away to school to study to become a teacher. My desire was to teach in Mono County.

In 1900 I returned to Bodie to teach, as Intermediate Teacher in the Grammar School, which employed three teachers.

In 1904 I married David Victor Cain, whose family had been prominent residents of Bodie since 1879. To him I owe much of the history I have written, and without his collaboration and help I could not have gone on with this story.

There was never a gathering of old timers, never a fireside group, that stories of the lawless days of the old camp were not told. Always the thought came to me, "Why should these tales die with the teller?" As I heard them over and over again (and each old timer had his favorite stories), I began to take notes, jot down funny incidents.

Later I began seriously to do some research work. I delved into the old files of the newspapers, the Coroner's records, lodge records, the Miners' Union books, and into the records in the county archives in Bridgeport.

In 1937 I had a severe and prolonged illness, from which I thought I might not recover. The unfinished story of Bodie was my greatest worry and concern. When I was able I wrote to George D. Lyman, who had been a classmate of mine in Nevada, and who had written that most successful and glamorous story, "The Saga of the Comstock Lode." I offered him all my material, if he would accept it and write the story of Bodie. He answered thus:

> "San Francisco, Calif.
> Sept. 10, 1937"

"Dear Ella:

"Your generous offer just reached me. No doubt you will recover from the coronary thrombosis. That will take time and patience. The convalescent period will be a good time for you to complete your story of Bodie. My roots are in Virginia City, yours are in Bodie, and I know you will do justice to the story. *Complete it.*

"I will be waiting with anticipation to read it when your book is published.

> "Most gratefully and sincerely yours,
> "GEORGE D. LYMAN"

So, at this late date, I have the material ready for the press.

I have tried to give you a true picture of the Bodie I knew. It is for you, who read this book, to judge whether or not Bodie deserved and sustained its reputation of being the most lawless, the wildest, and toughest mining camp the Far West has ever known.

ELLA M. CAIN

Contents

Introduction

This is the first book ever to be published about Bodie and its environs. It came to be printed and issued in a very interesting way.

In mid-Summer, 1953, Archie Stevenot of Sonora was in Mono County. He happened to call on Mrs. Ella Cain, as his sister had known her for years. Out of that conversation Archie learned that Mrs. Cain had recently completed a manuscript that was concerned with the history and life of the old ghost town of Bodie. Thus Mrs. Cain and her manuscript came to my attention.

During the Fall of 1953 I talked with Mrs. Cain several times and induced her to allow me to make the effort to see that her manuscript, and a portion of her fine collection of photographs, were put into print. I felt that her background as a lifelong resident of Bodie, and her years of school teaching, well qualified her to tell the story of one of the most fabulous mining camps that ever existed in the Old West.

Now, as Mrs. Cain's book comes from the press, it is more than coincidental that the California State Legislature has passed a bill, signed into law by Governor Goodwin J. Knight. It allows for funds to establish the ghost town of Bodie as an Historical Park unit of the California State Park System.

I am very pleased to have had a hand in the book and the effort put forth to establish Bodie State Park. Both of them will preserve history first-hand for generations to come.

It shall forever be to Mrs. Cain's glory that she struggled against almost impossible odds to save these valuable links with the colorful past of Mono County.

DONALD I. SEGERSTROM

Sonora, California
May 1, 1956

CHAPTER ONE

The Story of William Bodey

On a hot July day in 1859 the forms of a trudging prospector and his burro were silhouetted against the sky on the ridge of a steep peak. The man paused, pulled on the worn rope to stop the burro, and knelt down to scan the earth as he had done hundreds of times before. He finally arose, took the prospecting pick from the saddle bag, and began to dig. Suddenly he exclaimed, "Say, old Peter, this looks like pay dirt at last, and, if it is, you know and I know we came a hell of a ways to find it."

He was a man about 5 feet 6 inches in height, light complexioned, with hair and mustache turning gray; and aged about 45 years. He had followed the gold rush to California, coming around "the Horn" in 1848, in the sloop Matthew Vassar. He was a Dutchman from Poughkeepsie, New York, named William S. Bodey. There he had left a family: a wife, a daughter of nineteen, and a son of seventeen—who was preparing to enter college. (His history was told by S. Cobb, his partner, and was published in the Chronicle of Nov. 3rd, 1879.)

That evening he panned the dirt as his three companions—Doyle, Garraty and Black Taylor, who had

1

crossed the mountains with him, via Sonora Pass,
looked on. To their amazement a long string of the
bright yellow metal lay coiling around the edge of the
pan. They slapped each other on the back, then threw
their hats in the air, and finally Doyle shouted, "Come
on, boys, we can't do any less than drink the last part
of the last bottle. We'll take our chances on a snake
bite to drink a toast to Bodey, and the best showing
we've seen on the Eastern slope of these Sierra Nevada
Mountains."

The four prospectors thought so well of their placer
prospect, in what they called Taylor Gulch, that they
built a cabin and established a camp near a spring of
bubbling cold water. This was afterwards known as
Pearson Spring, and is a little northwest of the present
town. (The site of Bodey's cabin has been shifted
around so much by the various writers, he must have
occupied as many cabins as Mark Twain did in Aurora.)

The winter of '59 came early and was severe. Bodey
and Taylor were alone in their little cabin in the gulch.
In November they found themselves getting short of
food, and had to go on foot to Monoville for supplies.
On the return trip they were overtaken by a blizzard
and lost their way. Only one who has experienced a
Bodie winter can realize the fury with which the blinding snow, driven by the wintry blast, can sweep those
barren slopes; nor can one imagine the depth of snow
which can pile up in the course of a few hours. The
miners lost their way. The packs on their backs became
burdensome. They left them one by one. Their safety
lay in staying together. Finally Taylor realized that
Bodey's strength was failing. He tried to encourage
him by saying that they were near home, that he could

recognize landmarks, but Bodey, who was now lagging behind, did not seem to hear. At last he fell exhausted in the snow. In the blinding blizzard Taylor had difficulty in even finding him. He groped in the snow banks, which were now waist deep, and called him by name. The wind caught his voice and it trailed off in a sort of wail. He finally stumbled on to Bodey's prostrate form, and, after several attempts, was able to lift it to his shoulders. He staggered on for a few hundred yards, but the wind and blinding snow held him back like a demon that was possessed. He finally laid Bodey in the snow, in order to rest and regain his own strength, but when he tried to lift him again it was impossible. Taylor wrapped a blanket around him, put his mouth close to Bodey's ear, and told him they were not far from the cabin and that he would soon come back. Struggling on blindly, he at last ran up against a stony cliff. He leaned against it for support. Then suddenly the fact that it was the black bluff which rose some little distance behind their cabin filtered into his benumbed brain. Some way, he never knew how, he eventually reached the cabin and staggered in. He kindled a fire, made coffee, and ate some food.

The thoughts of Bodey out there in the snow were driving him mad. Putting on some dry clothing, he opened the door and again plunged into the fury of the storm. All night long he hunted for his companion, and called him by name, but no answer came back excepting the moan of the mocking wind.

In the morning he staggered back exhausted to the cabin. It continued to snow the next day — and the next. On the third day, when the storm finally cleared, and the snow lay like a blanket deep and white over the

mountains, no telltale spot disclosed the place where
Bodey's body lay buried. It remained for the prowling,
hungry coyotes to find it; even before spring, and when
Taylor at last came upon the spot, only naked bones,
bowie knife, pistol and blanket told him at last he
had found the place where his companion and friend
had perished. Reverently he buried him where he had
found him, wrapping all that remained of him and his
belongings in the blanket. He made a mound of earth
above him and placed a large boulder at the head as a
marker. How little he dreamed his own fate would be
more tragic than that of the companion he had buried.

With a heavy heart he returned to the diggings. It
was "uphill work" mining alone. The thoughts of
Bodey haunted him. In the dead of night the wind
howling around the cabin seemed to carry Bodey's last
cry for help to his ears. He decided to seek new fields.
After prospecting around Monoville, Dog Town, and
the other places where miners were working, he drifted
south to the little settlement of Benton.

He again took up his abode in a lonely cabin. Benton
was the gathering place for the hostile Paiute tribe,
who were attracted there by the hot springs which
gushed forth from volcanic formations. One night when
they were on the warpath they broke into Taylor's
cabin. Although taken unaware, he grabbed his gun
from above his bed and fought them back with the
ferocity of a tiger. When his ammunition was exhausted he used the butt of his gun, and not until *ten*
savages lay dead on the floor was he finally taken. They
then dragged him outside into the moonlight, and amid
savage yells severed his head from his body.

So was the miners' superstition of tragic deaths for

the discoverers of worthwhile camps borne out again.

The name of Bodey was almost forgotten, as the little camp that was destined later to bear his name sank into oblivion. Prospectors came and prospectors went, but the attention of the mining world was centered first on Virginia City and later on Aurora.

Finally in 1879, when the Standard and Bodie Con mines had made mining history, and ten thousand people called the gulch their home, suddenly an awakened interest and sentiment for the founder of the camp sprang into being. The spelling of the name of the camp had some way been changed to Bodie.

There was one dispute after another, in the papers of that day, as to where the remains of Bodey were actually buried. This disagreement was settled by J. G. McClinton, who had inadvertently stumbled upon the grave in 1871, while searching for his horse. In the fall of 1879, the boom year of Bodie, McClinton and Joseph Wasson together exhumed the remains. The Chronicle of Nov. 3, 1879, has the following article in regard to what happened:

"On Sunday last Judge McClinton and Joe Wasson went to the grave of William S. Bodey and commenced exhuming the remains of the pioneer whose name is bestowed upon the town of Bodie. The remains having been discovered, operations were suspended until the following day, when, in the presence of several citizens, they were removed and brought to town. The much mooted question as to the location of the grave has thus been settled. There was found the skull, a few bones, gun, necktie, bowie knife, shoe button, blanket and cloth. His remains will be reinterred tomorrow afternoon at 3 o'clock, under the auspices of the Pacific

Coast Pioneers of Bodie. A general invitation is extended to citizens to attend.''

The Chronicle of Nov. 8, 1879, tells of the funeral as follows:

"On Sunday last the remains of William S. Bodey were reinterred under the auspices of the Pacific Coast Pioneers of Bodie at 2 o'clock. The remains were placed in the Masonic Hall, where they were reviewed by a large number of citizens and ladies. All work was suspended for the day, and the Miners' Union members walked in the funeral procession. At the grave President B. B. Jackson introduced the Honorable R. D. Ferguson, who delivered the funeral oration. He did not dwell upon Bodey's character further than to state that he was a man of that indomitable pluck and energy which led him up these steep slopes in winter, when the blasts of a wintry sky, chill and frozen, were too severe for his powerful constitution and rigorous manhood; that he fell, wrapped in winter's snowy mantle, away from friends and home, with no loving hands to smooth his fevered brow, or soft eyes of affection to tenderly beam upon him or cheer the agony of his departing spirit. He went on further to say, 'Let him repose in peace on this lofty summit amid these everlasting hills; here where he blazed the trail and marked the first footprints to our golden peaks. Let a fitting and enduring monument be reared in his memory. Let it be wrought from the chiseled granite of these mountains. Let its shaft rise high above with sculptured urn o'ertopping, with the simple name of Bodey there to kiss the first golden rays of the coming sun, and where his setting beams may linger in cloudless majesty and beauty, undisturbed forever.' ''

And so the citizens of Bodie, fired with enthusiasm, and full of gratitude to the discoverer of their now booming camp, subscribed a fund of five hundred dollars to erect the very monument the Honorable R. D. Ferguson had described.

Some time in the latter part of 1880 a sculptor was brought to Bodie for the sole purpose of chiseling out of the native granite of the Bodie hills the majestic shaft described by the orator. Even the "sculptured urn" adorned its top, and now it was in readiness for the inscription.

But the bones of William Bodey might well rattle in their second grave at the fickleness of human nature.

When the news of the death of President Garfield reached Bodie, sentiment ran so high that the citizens agreed to place an inscription on Bodey's monument —to the memory of their martyred President. And so

The cemetery, Bodie, California

it stands, in the Masonic Cemetery in Bodie, to this day, bearing the inscription "ERECTED TO THE MEMORY OF JAMES A. GARFIELD." While further up on the hill in a grave overgrown with sagebrush, and unmarked, lie the remains of one William S. Bodey.

CHAPTER TWO

Development of the Mines
and the Growth of the Camp
in Riches and Lawlessness

From the day William Bodey made his first placer location, until Bodie took its place among the real gold camps of the Far West, there was a long drawn out, and, at times, a disappointing struggle.

A scarcity of water made it impossible to wash the placer deposits, and this led to a prospecting for quartz ledges. In August of 1859 the first quartz ledge was located, the claim being named the Montauk, later to be known as the Goodshaw. This location was directly above the place where Bodey had discovered the placer ground.

These first claims were recorded in Mono District. On July 10th, 1860, the miners of "Bodey Diggings" met and organized the Bodey Mining District, and adopted a set of laws by which they would be governed. Some of these laws were elastic to say the least—for instance, Article 6 reads:

"All persons holding claims in this district shall do

one day's work every week on said claim when there is sufficient water to work with an arrastra, or rocker."

"ARTICLE 11."

"Any person, or persons, discovering a quartz ledge shall be entitled to one extra claim for discovery."

"ARTICLE 12."

"All claims in this district shall be laid out and not be forfeited from the 1st day of October, 1860, until the 1st day of May, 1861."

The quartz claims located were two hundred fifty feet in length, with fifty feet on each side of quartz lode allowed for right of work.

Jeremiah Tucker was elected recorder for the term of one year.

The spelling of *Bodey* District is found throughout the mining records until October 15, 1862, when, on the Notice of Location of The Seneca Quartz Lode, the name *Bodie* appears for the first time. W. A. Chalfant tells, in his "Outposts of Civilization," that the spelling was changed by a sign painter, Bob Howland by name, who was ordered to paint a sign in Aurora for a livery stable owned by Bob Hazelton of the Body Ranch. He painted "BODIE STABLES" and, as the spelling was more pleasing, and there could be no doubt as to the pronunciation, it remained *Bodie* from that time on.

The most important location of any made in this camp, then in swaddling clothes, was the one dated July 1, 1861, when O. G. Leach, E. Donahue, and L. H. Dearborn located the Bunker Hill Mine, later to be called The Standard, on the eastern slope of Bodie Bluff. It looked so promising they soon sold out their interests for twenty thousand dollars to an actor named

James Stark, and his partner, a jeweler named John W. Tucker, both of whom had been mining in Aurora.

Stark owned an opera house in San Jose, and conceived the idea that it could be used to advantage in this new venture in Bodie. But the job of transporting it to the latter place, and transforming acoustics built for Patti into the framework for a quartz mill, was a sad experience for actor Stark and jeweler Tucker. They soon ran out of money, and were forced to sell their "Opera House Mill" to The Aurora Company.

A consolidation of different claims was resorted to in March, 1863, and a new company was formed, bringing in outside men and capital. Leland Stanford, who was then Governor of the State, was named President, and Judge F. T. Bechtel, who had been mining in Aurora, was elected Secretary. The new company was called the Bodie Bluff Consolidated Mining Company, and was incorporated for over a million dollars. (Mining Records—Book B.)

The Governor paid a visit to the camp, and actually stood within a few feet of millions in gold, but got discouraged and declared he would not give five hundred dollars for the whole district. His "Expert" had told him they could not raise a color 200 feet below the surface; if they did they could hang him in the shaft. Therefore, the Governor moved his mill away. This was in '73. A few years later, in '79, Leland Stanford came back to the now booming town, declared that he had missed a big fortune by acting on the advice of his so-called "Expert," who was nowhere in evidence—to be hanged in the shaft.

After Governor Stanford had decided to abandon this seemingly worthless mining ground, it passed into the hands of four men, who were without funds, namely, Essington, Lockberg, Mooney and Walker. They tried to develop it with much brawn and little capital. Again it was a failure.

Mooney and Walker finally had to quit the partnership. Mooney was afterwards elected to the State Legislature. Walker lost his life in a mine accident. Essington and Lockberg went on working the claim. They had found a good friend in the proverbial "Nigger in the Woodpile," one William O'Hara, an Irishman by name, an African by birth.

O'Hara ran a boarding house; and Essington and Lockberg ate there, until they finally owed O'Hara board and borrowed money to the tune of nine hundred and fifty dollars. They were struggling to develop the mine, and worked the ore from the claim in an arrastra. The Negro, O'Hara, acted as watchman of the mine at night, and as a restaurant keeper by day. Finally the Scandinavians decided they were in deep enough, turned the mine over to O'Hara for the $950.00 they owed him, and left camp.

In vain, the colored gentleman offered to let anybody who would, take over the mine, "on time," for the money he was out. They could even pay him out of the ore as milled. *There was no one forthcoming.*

Essington and Lockberg, after drifting around other camps, and finding nothing as promising as the Standard, came back to Bodie in 1874. They took O'Hara up on the proposition to work out the debt, and again began digging and hoping. Timber for the workings was scarce and expensive, and this resulted in a lucky break for them. One day a rumble and a roar told them the ground was caving in, and when they went, quite disheartened, to see the extent of the damage to their workings, a veritable Aladdin's Cave stood exposed to their view. There it was with its golden treasure; the ledge they had *dreamed* of, had *worked* for, had *hoped* to find; its richness exceeding even their wildest expectations. Dame fortune had embraced them with open arms.

During the next two seasons Essington and Lockberg, cleaned up a nice little "nest egg" from the old arrastra in the gulch. Deciding that a mill was necessary, but, not wanting to build it with the $37,000 they had taken from their "Aladdin's Cave," they decided to sell. This time they asked the handsome figure of $75,000 for the property. When, in 1876, Seth and Dan Cook, John Boyd and William Lent offered them $67,500 in cash for it, they sold.

The Standard Company was incorporated in April, 1877, with a capital of 50,000 shares, at $100 a share, making a total capitalization of five million dollars. Dan Cook was elected President, John F. Boyd Vice President, and William Irwin Superintendent. The main office was Nevada Block, San Francisco. These men became rich. John Boyd bought a big estate in Marin County, California; William Irwin erected the Irwin Hotel in San Francisco, and William Lent also invested his money in the Bay City.

The first ores milled by this new company were treated at the Syndicate Plant, but the Standard owners soon started the erection of a twenty-stamp mill of their own, part of the machinery being brought from the Del Monte mill below Aurora. A tramway was built from mine to mill, and as the tiny buckets moved along incessantly on their endless chain up and down the hill,

they sang a song of *gold gold gold,* which was heard
around the world, and, in 1878, the rush for Bodie
was on.

They came from the nearby camp of Aurora, from
Virginia City, which was now on the decline, from the
Mother Lode, from "The City by the Golden Gate,"
from all points of the compass, spurred on by the tales
of fabulous riches to be found on the top of the world—
in the mining camp of Bodie.

The highways and byways were congested with all
sorts and manners of vehicles, stage coaches, twenty-
mule teams, pack trains, dead-ax wagons, lumber teams,
fruit wagons from Tuolumne, via the Sonora Pass,
weary prospectors — trudging along beside heavily
loaded burros, gamblers—buggies drawn by spirited
horses, all on-rushers bent on being among the first to
ply their trade in the new found gold camp.

The Bodie stage line ran eight stages regularly, with

Part of town of Bodie—1879

fifty-four horses—six stationed at each of the nine stops.

Bodie, which from 1860 to 1877 had polled a vote of only twenty, in 1879 rose to an estimated population of from ten to twelve thousand; as miners, gamblers, business men, prostitutes and speculators swept into town.

The discovery of new leads in the Bodie mine, and the further development of The Standard, caused a sudden rise in values in the camp. Stock in the Bodie Mining Company catapulted from 50c to $54 a share. Gold was so plentiful, and the supply so inexhaustible, that there followed a few of the wildest, maddest years the West has ever known.

The sky was the limit in gambling, drinking and

Bodie Miners' Union Hall

shooting. Bodie was often called "Shooters' Town."
It was more advertised for its lawlessness than for the
wealth of its mines. The popular greeting as the miners
met in the morning was, "Have we a man for breakfast
this morning?"

However, the call of gold had been answered, too, by
thousands of good, substantial, respectable people.
Hundreds of comfortable, while not pretentious, homes

Methodist Church

had been built to the east and west of Main Street. The town was well laid out, and every street was named.

In 1878 the Miners' Union built a fine, big hall, which was used throughout long years for lodge meetings, shows, dances, and even for funerals. Many a fine grand ball was held in this hall, which still stands and now houses the Museum exhibit.

Two churches were built: a Catholic church on the eastern slope, whose first Pastor was Father Cassin; and a quaint Methodist church, which still stands and was presided over by Reverend Hinkle, a quiet scholarly man, not unlike the Minister in Goldsmith's "Deserted Village." These two churches had small congregations, considering the population of the camp, but the children were taught to faithfully attend Sunday School. They had heard so much of the wild camp to which their parents were taking them, that a newspaper editor in Truckee, California, printed the prayer of a little girl, which read: "Good-bye God! I'm going to Bodie." The editor of the Bodie paper replied by saying that the little girl had been grossly misquoted, that what she had really said was: "Good, by God! I'm going to Bodie."

The birth of the first white child was recorded in 1865—"To the wife of Robert Horner, a daughter."

In 1879 Bodie had reached its pinnacle. The main street was over a mile long, built solidly with one and two story frame buildings. Nearly every other business house was a saloon and gambling hall.

The first newspaper, "The Standard Pioneer Journal of Mono County," was published October 10th, 1877, by Frank Kanyon, Editor. It started as a weekly and was soon edited as a tri-weekly.

A telegraph line was built about this time (via Bridgeport) connecting Genoa, Nevada, and Bodie. The first dispatch read, "Bodie sends greetings—and proclaims to the mining world that her gold mines are the most wonderful yet discovered." This message was copied widely by all newspapers in Nevada and western California.

Whisky sold for two drinks for a quarter, or 10c by the single drink. No man was more despised than the one who would frequently lay his "short bit" on the bar for a solitary drink. He was promptly named "Short Dime Bill," or "Short Bit Pete." The call, "Fire in the Head," in a saloon, meant everybody drink. So those who often "treated the house" were dubbed "Fire in the Head Kelley," or "Fire in the Head Jones" (*That* was a title of distinction.) Plenty of whisky was consumed day and night. It was found to be as good for warding off pneumonia as for snake bites. It was shipped into the camp a hundred barrels at a time, by freight teams. The drivers of the twenty-mule teams got theirs enroute. They would hammer up the iron hoop of a barrel, drive in a nail, pull it out, and place their jugs under the little stream that gushed forth. The hole was then plugged up with a sliver of wood, the hoop hammered back into place, and the theft would defy detection. As the roads were mighty dusty, the driver would feel the need of "wetting his whistle" often, so that when he finally reached town he was so drunk he would actually tumble off the driver's seat into the corral yard.

Quarrels in the saloons were frequent, and often accompanied by gun play, but these were not taken seriously by the community which had grown accus-

Pat Reddy

tomed to "having a man for breakfast" every morning.
However, the time came when gun play was not con-
fined to the sporting element, and the "respectable citizens" realized something had to be done about it.

Pat Reddy, the able criminal lawyer, had become the
bulwark for this hardened shooting element, and generally got his man off "Scot free." A drunken teamster
named Draper beat his wife to death with a black
snake, threw her body out of the wagon, and rode away
leaving her remains on the Bodie-Lundy road. He
pleaded self defense, and was given only a seven-year
sentence.

In the town of Bridgeport, Henry Robbins had been
shot by George Hawkins, and died in Bodie from the
effects of the wounds four weeks later. Hawkins was
exonerated.

"Bad Mike," a notorious character of Bodie's underworld, stabbed a poor half-wit of the town, in cold
blood, in front of a store on Main Street. Mike, by
reason of his pull with the gambling element, was sentenced to only two years in San Quentin.

Then one night, during a dance in the Miners' Union
Hall, a crime was enacted that caused even Bodie to sit
up and take notice. A Cornish woman, by the name of
Mrs. Treloar, was seen to be dancing frequently with a
Frenchman named Joseph DeRoche. Her husband was
not present, as he was working night shift in the mine.
Gossip had it that DeRoche, who had built an impos-
ing two-story brick home in Bodie, and who was a
bachelor, was seen frequently at the humble home of
Johnny Treloar, across the street, while the latter was
away at work. Treloar was a mild mannered "Cousin
Jack," but had frequently quarreled with his wife

about the attentions of DeRoche. On the night of this dance, January 14th, 1881, he had forbidden his wife to dance with DeRoche, and on coming into the hall after shift, about midnight, had found her in the arms of the Frenchman. He walked up to the couple, and, putting a detaining hand on his wife, asked her to come home; whereupon DeRoche requested that he step outside with him and they would talk things over. They had walked about sixty feet up Main Street when DeRoche was seen, by two witnesses, to put his hand in his hip pocket, pull out a gun, put it against Treloar's head and pull the trigger. Treloar, who was unarmed, dropped, a bleeding mass, into the snow. He died almost instantly.

DeRoche immediately engaged Pat Reddy to defend him. Pat exacted as his fee everything DeRoche possessed. It was granted. There was talk of lynching, so Reddy had DeRoche removed from jail, as a safeguard against the mob, and taken to the Bon Ton Lodging House, under guard of Deputy Sheriff Farnsworth. That night DeRoche escaped, "presumably" while Farnsworth was asleep. When the infuriated citizens heard it they organized the "601 Vigilante Committee."

A posse, led by a prominent businessman of the town, apprehended DeRoche at the "Goat Ranch," eight miles from Bodie. This ranch had seemed the likely place to find him, as it was owned by French Canadians. A vote was taken there to determine whether DeRoche should be lodged in the County Jail at Bridgeport for trial or taken back to Bodie. By a majority of just *one* vote, it was decided that he be returned to Bodie. This sealed his fate.

In the meantime Officer Farnsworth, who had seen

the handwriting on the wall, decided to shake the dust of Bodie from his heels. He was never heard of afterwards.

When the posse returned with DeRoche, they placed him, heavily guarded, in the jail for several hours.

The "601," after holding a mass meeting, went to Wilson Butler's blacksmith shop, which was back of the Miners' Union Hall, and, by manpower alone, carried a huge wagon crane that was used to lift the beds off heavy wagons for repairs, and brought it to the spot where the blood of Treloar still stained the snow.

At this point they were interrupted by the toughs of the town, who had organized a "Law and Order Party" under the direction of an attorney whose business it was to defend hardened criminals. A lawyer, who had formerly been Attorney General of Nevada, put up a strenuous voice against the hanging that seemed to be imminent. "Get a rope and we'll hang you," shouted young Billy Metson, who himself was afterwards a prominent attorney in San Francisco. The move seemed to meet with such hearty approval that the lawyer took Deputy Sheriff Farnsworth's hunch and left town without delay.

About midnight, all arrangements being completed, DeRoche was led silently from the jail to where the scaffold stood in readiness. A noose was placed around his neck, and he was heard to say "Oh! My God." About twenty men took hold of the rope, and pulling on it, slowly walked away, while the body twisted and writhed in mid air. At dawn the body was cut down and sent to the undertaking parlors of Charlie Kelley. There DeRoche was laid out with the hangman's rope lying coiled on his chest like a snake, as a warning to other would-be bad characters.

An investigation into the death of DeRoche was made. Billy Metson once told me that the man who tied the noose and the leader of the "601" were both on the jury. The case against DeRoche was closed on the Justice of the Peace record with the brief sentence, "Case dismissed, as the defendant was taken out and hanged by a mob."

(DeRoche's two-story brick house was later used as a County Hospital.)

Not long after this lynching Pat Reddy was challenging jurors on a murder trial at the County Seat, when he asked a talesman if he would object to having the list of the Bodie "601" read, he replied, "Certainly not, Mr. Reddy. My name is listed opposite No. 27, and if you have a copy of the Minutes of that Organization you can read where one Pat Reddy is considered as being dangerous to the community, and one who will probably receive an invitation from the '601' to start traveling if his mode of life does not change." Thereafter Reddy was careful to make no further mention of the "601."

The lynching of DeRoche, while it had a quieting effect on the bad element of the camp, did not suppress gun play. Five days after DeRoche was buried, in "Boot Hill," the Coroner's records show that one David Banner was killed by H. Ryan, and states it was "A quarrel between sporting men."

Shortly afterwards Officer Roberts killed J. E. Meyers, in self defense. This was quickly followed by David Mitchell being killed by James Stockdale in an opium den.

The dens of Chinatown played no minor role in the killings that went on. Bodie's Chinatown was typical of the ones you would find in San Francisco, Sacramento, or even in the homeland itself. The Chinese have a knack of reproducing their oriental atmosphere even to the smells—anywhere they settle. Their main street ran at a right angle to the Bodie Main Street. It was narrow and lined on each side by little wooden shacks, with here and there an imposing two or three story building housing a "Mercantile Establishment." The largest of the latter was a General Mercantile business owned by "Tong" Sing Wo, the big Tong boss of Chinatown.

No effort was made in most places to conceal the opium bunks. They were on the street floor, and spectators going up and down the streets could look into places where men, and women too, were lying in bunks smoking opium, while others sat around a table in the same room playing faro, fan-tan, and other Chinese gambling games. The windows were dingy, and partially covered with little red strips of paper on which was Chinese writing.

During the Chinese New Years Festival the streets were thronged with white people, and the Chinese were most lavish in giving gifts of native candy, nuts, tangerines and spiced fruits, to all visitors. To the places up town, like the bank and Wells Fargo, where they did business, they brought gifts of fine Satsuma, Royal Canton, Cloisonne, and other beautiful wares and embroidered silks, as "Happy New Year presents."

The "Chinks" of Bodie did little mining, even on the placers. They ran laundries, peddled vegetables and fruits (shipped in by express), and brought in and sold all the wood used in the camp. Every day large pack trains of burros came into town carrying in iron racks, on their sides, the nut pine wood that was brought from a great distance. They were herded by two or three "Chinks," who carried long poles, and who kept up a continuous yelling, and perhaps swearing, in their native language. This singsong could be heard for half a mile away, and at times grew more emphatic, when a herder would pick up a rock and land it on the back of a donkey that had gotten out of line, or stopped to graze by the roadside.

Centrally located in Chinatown was a Chinese Temple or Joss House. On the altar was a large bronze figure of Confucius, surrounded by statues of the lesser gods. When Chinatown was abandoned in later years, Confucius saw no more worshipers bowing down before him; but an unscrupulous Jewish junk gatherer gave a couple of local boys 50c to sell him the bronze idol, and Confucius went out of town on the top of a load of junk.

Adjoining Chinatown to the north was the "Red Light District." Above every door hung a little red light, the trademark and badge of shame of its occupant. The "girls" were seldom seen on the Main Street of town in the daytime, but frequented most of the saloons at night. In some places they danced with the miners.

In his article, "The Bodie That Was," Carl P. Russel has the following to say:

That "the bad *girls* from Bodie were not far behind the bad men in extending their reputations, which may be judged by the following item from The Prospect (paper) of Silver Cliff, Colorado, September, 1880:

" 'A bad *girl* from Bodie with a split in her ear ar-

rived yesterday. She comes in search of a gay deceiver.'
If the gay deceiver was in Silver Cliff she undoubtedly
found him. The same girl went to Leadville, and was
there only two days when she mashed a hotel proprietor
and got $800 out of him. She then took in a mining
man, and duped him to the tune of about $1,000, besides
raising the devil with his family. A bad Bodie girl is
bad in the extreme, especially when under the influence
of whisky."

The two main streets of the "Red Light District"
were called Maiden Lane and Virgin Alley.

Rosa May of "The Highgrade," Emma Goldsmith
of "The Ozark," "Madame Mustache," and more recently a girl called "The Beautiful Doll" were the most
glamorous and most notorious. The demimondes frequented the saloons only at night, and came arrayed in
the most glamorous styles of the time.

Bodie had among its ten thousand people its good
and its bad. We can say with Shakespeare:

"The evil that men do lives after them,
The good is oft interred with their bones."

So "The Bad Man from Bodie" still carries his guns
and his bowie knives down through history in the
chronicles of the wild exciting life of the Gold Rush
days.

Further on you may read Jim Pender's stories of the
virtuous and the wicked, who walked across the stage
and played their parts in the drama enacted in this
rip-roaring mining camp on the top of the world.

CHAPTER THREE

Bodie Cemetery and Boot Hill

Paradoxical as it may seem, there is more life in the Bodie cemetery in summer days than in any other place in town. The tourists swarm in from the different resorts of Mono County to visit the famous "Boot Hill" of the old lawless mining camp. They wander among the tumbling headstones and neglected graves, hoping to find the last resting place of "The Bad Man from Bodie." They do not know that the real "Boot Hill" lies below the main cemetery on the downward slope,

Bodie cemetery and Boot Hill

outside the fence, outside the pale of decency as it were.

The people of the camp sat in judgment on the lives of those who passed away, to determine whether they merited burial in the respectable cemetery, or should be relegated to "Boot Hill." This led to feuds that were often settled by gun play. Thus it was brought about that "Boot Hill" opened its nefarious mouth to receive two or three bodies instead of one.

Seldom, if ever, were any markers put on the graves outside the fence. Why should all who came, know of their disgrace? Sometimes a wooden fence enclosed a grave, as is the case with Rosa May, the demimonde. Hers is a pathetic, weather-beaten little picket fence now leaning crazily to the north. The grave of her lover, Ernest Marks, beside hers, is now only a hollow depression in the earth.

Here, also, are the graves of James DeRoche, who was strung up by the Vigilante Committee for the

Grave of Rosa May

killing of Thomas Treloar; of David Banner, killed in
a saloon row between "sporting men"; of Neva Pine,
who died from an overdose of opium (August 9, 1881);
of Harry Robbins, killed by William Hawkins; of
James Kennedy, killed by James Baker (July 7, 1880);
of Charlie Jardine, shot through the heart by "Pioche"
Kelley; of David Mitchell, killed in an opium den
(June 7, 1880); of two suicides, Chester W. Mills and
Robert Stevens; of Jim Desmond, who died with his
boots on in a saloon row; of Felix DeGuirre, alias
Donnelly, who murdered William Deegan and Patrick
Coyle; of "Peek-a-boo" Patten, a sporting woman; of
James Madden, slain in the Palace Laurel Saloon by
an officer; of Henry Chatterton, who died of exposure
while drunk; and so the list could go on and on.

Scattered here and there is a small neglected grave,
the resting place of an illegitimate child. Some of the
forebears of these children had family plots above, on
the *hill with the fence;* but that did not matter, the rul-
ing of the camp was inexorable.

Above the main cemetery, on the upper slope to the
west, and again *outside the fence,* were the graves of
several hundred Chinese. This was a matter of race
prejudice. The "Mother Lode" had experienced the
threat of Coolie labor and the Chinese Exclusion Act
had been passed in 1882.

The Chinese funerals were conducted with great cere-
mony and ancient tradition. Thousands of little red
papers were scattered along the route of the funeral
procession. The devil would have to pick all these bits
of paper up before he could overtake and *possess* the
deceased. The latter would by this time be well on his
way to heaven. Quantities of food, including the tradi-

tional roast pork, were placed on the grave; and here
let it be said that the Paiute Indians were not long in
discovering this fact. Many a feast of roast pork and
other foods was held in the Indian camps on the out-
skirts of town soon after a Chinese funeral. Years
afterward, the bones of these Chinese were exhumed
and shipped back to China; the Chinese belief being
that the deceased, in order to attain the celestial regions
permanently, must be buried in the soil of their homeland.

Within the fence the large monument with the inscription "Erected to the memory of James A. Garfield" is easily the most imposing shaft of any in the
three different sections of the righteous burying
ground. That it was intended to be erected over the
grave of William S. Bodey, the discoverer of the camp,
is told in his story elsewhere.

Many have remarked, after reading the inscriptions
on the headstones, that the percentage of children
buried here seemed to be very large. This, however, is
not the case. The fact is that the mortality among
children was not unnecessarily high, but that the be-
reaved parents usually placed a lasting monument over
a child's grave.

In the more recent bootlegging days, a hollow bronze
monument with the name Pagden on it was used as a
cache for liquor. The bootlegger, coming into town
under cover of darkness, would proceed to the cemetery,
and by unscrewing a bronze plate on the back of the
monument would pack the hollow monument with bottles of liquor. When the saloon keeper took them away
he would leave the wherewithal to pay for them.

Most tourists now labor up the steep slope to get to

the grave of Lottie, the last grave in the upper cemetery, with its pretentious iron railing. They heard of Lottie, whom the self-righteous of another day were wont to shun. They have seen her picture, with the kind expression, the smiling lips, and the laughing eyes. If you read her story farther on, would you say that she was the Magdalen of Bodie?

The great percentage of other headstones were just wooden slabs and have long since gone to decay, leaving hundreds of graves without any mark whatsoever. An epidemic of diphtheria, in the 80's, took a heavy toll among the children, but the disease most dreaded by everyone was pneumonia. During the severe winters when the thermometer registered 30 to 40 degrees below zero, many a miner who worked his shift one day was dead the next, stricken down by this swift and fatal malady. The intense cold, the poorly heated houses, the treatment of the disease, were all contributing factors to its deadliness. The people always spoke of these severe cold spells as being "real pneumonia weather."

In winter when the snow was lying at a depth of from seven to ten feet, with perhaps a blizzard still raging, a funeral had to be delayed for several days. The ground would be frozen so hard that giant powder had to be used to loosen the frozen earth. At regular intervals the dull thud of the exploding powder could be heard all over the town, accompanied by a trembling of the earth and a rattling of windows. If an epidemic happened to be raging at the time, these dull blasts would strike foreboding and terror into the hearts of the people in this snowbound and isolated outpost of civilization.

During one severe winter the Superintendent of the

Standard Mine, and therefore the most important and
prominent citizen of the camp, died. His body had to
lie in his residence for nearly two weeks. From then
on all heavy winters were compared to "the winter
when Pettibone died."

Often it was found to be impossible to break a road
to the cemetery on account of the depth of the snow and
the frightful blizzards. Many a body had to be taken
to its last resting place on a wooden sled, drawn through
the snow by sorrowing friends. Of course, at other
seasons when weather and roads permitted, one of the
two horsedrawn hearses pictured here was used.

They are still in a good state of preservation, and are
quite as pretentious as any that were to be found in a
large city. The sides are plate glass, the trappings
etched silver. Inside one, at the farthest end, is a painting of "The Open Door." Huge feather plumes adorn
the tops, held in place by silver urns. They were kept

for years in the brick building below the cemetery, but have since been moved to the Cain Museum, where they can now be seen.

The hearses were available to saint and sinner alike, providing the rental of $20 was forthcoming. A Chinaman who had lost his wife came to the undertaker one day to rent "the glassy wagon with the feather dusters." He rented it with the proviso that all the edibles be transported in a separate vehicle.

A description of the Bodie cemetery would not be complete without some mention of the undertakers who conducted the funerals and generally drove the hearse. There seemed to be no special qualifications needed to act in this capacity, save an aptitude and the hanging out of one's shingle. From the early day directories and bill heads, it is to be inferred that undertaking was generally a side line to some other business.

"Shotgun" Johnnie Heilshorn was a Cornish undertaker who carried out all the traditions of Bodie's bad men. At the close of the funeral services Johnnie would

arise and give forth his final instruction: "Come ye forth, all ye wee Nickies and ye big Nickies, come forth and take a geek at he before I screw 'im down." This invitation was accepted with all solemnity. Johnnie was an undertaker by trade, a rounder by profession, a thief by inclination, a dope fiend by choice, and a scalawag by association. The main scalawag of his association was one "Big Bill" Monahan, whose reputation was as bad and black as himself. "Shotgun" Johnnie had a habit of saying, "The prop's this," or "The prop's that" (prop was slang for proposition). One night he and "Big Bill" held up a stable man at the point of sawed-off guns, but when on searching him they failed to find any money, the smaller masked robber spoke up and said, "The prop's to go through 'im again," and the stable man knew instantly who was behind that mask. However, a jury failed to bring in a verdict of guilty, so Johnnie and Bill went, with still greater confidence, on their road of crime.

One night the matron of the County Hospital, which was built near the graveyard, heard some disturbance in the cemetery. On looking out she saw two men carrying a casket away from the burying ground and entering the Heilshorn Morgue; this is the brick building near Boot Hill. Investigators found that a newly made grave seemed to be somewhat caved in, and on digging down the body was found wrapped only in a sheet. Johnnie and Bill were again brought to trial, and again acquitted, as the sorrowing relatives could not identify the casket which had been stolen. Johnnie's shop contained many of the same type. However, after this incident, "Shotgun" noticed that his business was falling away. He had no customers, either for his new, and much less for his second hand coffins.

Johnnie was seen more and more frequently in the "joints" around Chinatown. Then one morning he was found dead in a Chinese bunk, presumably from an overdose of opium or morphine, or both. He was his own last customer for a coffin, first or second hand.

Following the Heilshorn and Monahan trial for grave robbing, many apprehensive relatives began having newly made graves opened, which resulted in a discovery that shook the camp, which was accustomed to nearly every form of crime, to its very foundation. The wife of a prominent citizen had died of an ailment that had baffled the two leading doctors of the town. They had tried to persuade the husband to let them perform an autopsy on the body to determine the cause of death. The husband had refused. When her grave was opened, coffin, body and all had disappeared. Suspicion pointed to the doctors, and feeling against them in the camp reached a white heat. There was talk of lynching, if enough evidence against the physicians could be secured. Then a counter sensation broke. A white figure, presumably of the dead woman, was seen to move back and forth at night on the side of a barn, in the vicinity of her former home. Thousands of people gathered to view the apparition. About the second night the two doctors made their get-away, and were never heard of afterwards. One deserted his wife and infant daughter. The wife finally divorced him, and moved to Nevada. Some time later it was whispered around that a magic lantern, operated from a two-story building by friends of the doctors, had made the "spook" walk. Bodie had thus been cheated of a double **lynching.**

The last of Bodie's bad men was "Two Gun Al." He always said he carried two guns because he didn't want to feel naked in Bodie. Al was never known to have killed a man, but he took part in many a shooting scrape. He used to say he didn't consider he had a good day if he didn't get into at least one fight. He was lodged in jail at numerous times, but his pals would go down with a bottle of whisky, and pour it into the tin cup which Al held through the barred jail windows. When the jailer returned, there old Al would be, dead drunk—but happy.

On one occasion he was lodged in jail when he rode into Ernest Mark's saloon on a horse, upset everything in the place, and took the swinging doors off their hinges on his departure.

At another time he made jail when he rode into an establishment in the "Red Light District," and insisted on tying his horse to a demimonde's grand piano.

Al was found dead in bed one morning, and was buried the same afternoon. . . . A local doctor's wife, who imbibed freely, complained that the doctor had not been called on to issue a death certificate, thereby losing a fee. She made the rounds of the saloons that night, declaring that Al had to be, by law, dug up, because he wasn't *"officially* dead"; but the people of Bodie decided to let him stay buried, "officially dead," or otherwise.

CHAPTER FOUR

History of the Camp up to the Present Time

Unlike Virginia City and Leadville, Colorado, Bodie was not built on a hillside. The townsite was on level ground, grassy in the places where it was not trampled off. The streets were well planned, and there was plenty of room even when the population was 10,000.

The view from any part of town is quite drab and desolate, as there is no vegetation excepting sagebrush.

Mono Lake

However, the view from the top of Bodie Bluff, on Standard Hill, is unsurpassed. To the southeast one sees the beautiful White Mountains, north of Bishop, California. The pastel colors of these mountains are ever changing, topped by white snowcaps on the peaks. To the south are seen the extinct craters of Mono Basin, and below—beautiful Mono Lake is an ever changing kaleidoscope of color. The fiery reds of sunset, the pastels of the rising sun, or the drab gray color of the tempest on a winter's day, are reflected in its bosom. To the southwest one can see the tallest peaks of the Sierras, Mt. Dana and Mt. Lyle, and the bench where the Tioga Pass leads into the Yosemite Park. Still farther west are the shadows of Lundy and Virginia Lake canyons, the latter at the base of majestic Black Mountain. Dunderberg Peak stands out like another Fujiyama, white capped, with a small forest nestled at its base. It is a panorama view, with a scope of over a hundred miles, the background being the loftiest peaks

Dunderberg Peak

of the Sierra Nevada Mountains, making a scene unsurpassed for the grandeur of its beauty.

Bodie is supplied with water by a mountain spring that rises at Potato Peak, four miles to the west. It is piped into town. This spring has never failed to gush forth, even in the driest years. The water is icy cold, and almost absolutely pure—by analysis. It is said that this pure water constituted the secret of the good beer made in Bodie in the early days. There were seven breweries in operation at one time, and beer in barrels was about the only load the big teams hauled on going out.

When the camp was raided by prohibition officers in 1929, the bootleg whisky was so good that, after they had sampled the evidence, they took plenty of evidence back with them. Heavy fines were imposed, but the "Prohis" weren't well over the hill when the saloons were running full blast again. Miners just can't work on soda pop.

In 1881 the crying need for lumber, timber and fuel for the Bodie mines led to the construction of a narrow gauge railroad, to tap the timber deposit south of Mono Lake, where a sawmill was already operating. The road was 32 miles in length, and was incorporated February, 1881, as the Bodie Railway Lumber Company, with a capital of $1,000,000; headquarters in San Francisco. The directors were H. M. Yerington (the railroad builder of Nevada), H. J. Ralston, R. M. Graves, W. S. Wood, J. B. Law, and J. M. Quay. The terminus was at Mono Mills. In 1880 Bodie had used 5,000,000 feet of lumber, which had been supplied by the lumber camp at Mono Mills, and four lumber mills in Bridgeport, which were running full blast; the

Twin Lakes, Robinson, Buckeye, and Yaney Canyon mills. Little attention had yet been given to farming in Bridgeport Valley, first known as Big Meadows, the quick turnover in lumber having been more attractive.

The lumber from the Mono Mills camp was floated in barges across Mono Lake. The finest and biggest barge was The Rocket, which had previously plied around the harbor at San Francisco. At the northeast part of Mono Lake the lumber was loaded on big teams and brought into Bodie. When the railroad to Mono Mills was at last completed, the people of Bodie put on a glorious celebration. At a given hour in the morning, every whistle in camp was turned on full blast. A procession was formed on Main Street, headed by the Miners' Union, followed by other organizations, and by the citizens, who marched up to the top of Reservoir Hill to the music of the Bodie Brass Band. The four engines had been stoked for full speed ahead; there

Mono Mills lumber train

were speeches and music and singing, and, after bottles of wine had been broken over them, christening them "The Mono," "The Inyo," "The Tybo," and "The Bodie," they steamed down the track with their bells ringing and their throttles wide open, while the on-lookers went wild with enthusiasm and delight. A more exciting demonstration could not have been witnessed.

About this time the name of J. S. Cain began to be prominently mentioned. He and Thomas Holt owned and operated the lumber barges on Mono Lake. Thomas Holt became the new Superintendent and General Manager of the Bodie Railroad & Lumber Company. Soon afterwards he and J. S. Cain took a lease on all its holdings. His daughter, Dolly, afterwards married E. W. Billeb, the last Superintendent and Manager of the Bodie Railroad.

At times 5,000 cords of wood were stored on the Standard Hill. Thirty-two hoists were operated by

Courthouse in Bridgeport, California

steam power. The consumption of wood in town, too, was tremendous, due to the rigors of the Bodie climate.

It was not uncommon during the winter for the snow to be 8 or 10 feet deep, and tunnels were dug along the sidewalks under the porches on Main Street, and across the street.

In 1880 the output from the mines had increased the tax payroll to such an extent that the Courthouse in Bridgeport was built. The foundation was of Bodie granite.

The Standard Mine, in 1881, paid in dividends to its stockholders $975,000. The total production of all mining done in Bodie, up to the present time, is estimated to be between 95 and 100 million.

In 1880 J. S. Cain and Joe Maguire obtained a six months lease on a block of ground in the Standard Mine. They worked three months without striking a pay chute, but in the next three months they took out $90,000. They had struck the fabulously rich Fortuna vein. Their lease was not renewed, and the Standard Company took millions out of this vein before it faulted.

Bodie laid claim to four unique features:

First: The wildest street of any mining camp.

Second: The wickedest men.

Third: The worst climate out of doors.

Fourth: The best water on earth.

During its history Bodie had two bad mine accidents. In July of '79 two tons of giant powder went off accidentally in the Summit Mine. Four miners lost their lives. The explosion was so tremendous that the whole town was shaken to its foundation. In 1880 the Goodshaw mine had a fire, which started in the hoisting works and spread to the shaft and then to the lower tunnels. Four poor fellows, working underground, lost their lives in this fire.

No scene is as heartrending as a mine fire, with wives, children, relatives, and friends standing helpless above, watching flames and smoke pouring out of a shaft where their loved ones are imprisoned below.

One of the hottest battles ever fought over a mining claim took place in August, 1879. There were two adjoining claims, the Jupiter and the Owyhee. The Owyhee claimed the Jupiter had infringed on their ground. George Daly, the Superintendent of the Jupiter, was blamed for the trouble, as it was thought he unjustly coveted the Owyhee ground. Paid gunmen were hired on each side, to defend their rights. The Owyhee fighters fought from a dugout, while the Jupiters used their hoisting works, which had been converted into a veritable fort. Finally a man was killed in the Owyhee dugout.

The Miners' Union, several hundred strong, took a hand in the fight. They marched up and took possession of the battleground. In the Jupiter fort they found a brother-in-law of Daly, mortally wounded. He died a few hours later in a rooming house in town. The populace called loudly for the arrest of George Daly as a claim jumper, and trouble maker, and thereby guilty of the deaths of these two men. Daly hired Pat Reddy to defend him, and again the Citizens' Committee, the "601" slipped in. They gave Daly and his gang 24 hours to leave town, but in much less time than that they shook the dust of Bodie from their feet.

Daly, always looking for trouble, later took part in the Geronimo Indian troubles in Arizona. He was killed by the Apache Indians, who were waiting in ambush as Geronimo and his band approached.

Late in 1881 the camp showed the first symptoms of a decline. The excitement of the gold rush had subsided. The lawless element had gone to seek more exciting fields, and disappointed people, who had not "grown rich quick," were leaving. Properties that had not "proven up" were being abandoned. The principal mines, like the Standard, Bodie, Noonday, Mono Syndicate, and a few others, were still big producers, and continued to be over a long term of years. There had been a sudden collapse of the Red Cloud, followed by a temporary shutting down of the Noonday. Both of these mines had sunk deep shafts on their properties. But Bodie was still a lively camp, with between four and five hundred men working. The wages ranged from $4.00 a day for miners to $5.00 and $6.00 for foremen and trained mechanics. On these wages, which to us today would seem only a pittance, whole families lived, and lived comfortably.

Two papers were being printed at this time, "The Daily Free Press" and "Weekly Standard," with Osborne and Cleveland as owners and editors.

The social activity of the camp centered around the fraternal organizations, of which there were many, the Masons, Odd Fellows, Ancient Order of United Workmen, the Miners' Union, Chosen Friends, Rebekahs, Knights of Pythias, Degree of Honor, Knights Templar, and Firemen's Organization. Each of these organizations gave a "Grand Ball" once a year, on the same date, chosing mostly the holidays in the different months. For instance, the Fourth of July was the date of the Miners' Union Grand Ball. On the 22nd of

February the Masonic dance was held. The Rebekahs
had their dance on September 20th, and so on. These
so-called "Grand Balls" were really elaborate affairs.
All the ladies dressed in evening clothes, in the mode of
the day, even to long kid gloves and fans. The men did
not wear tuxedos, but made a very creditable appearance. The grand march formed promptly at 9 o'clock.
It was led by the head officer of the lodge giving the
dance, and his lady. Elaborate dance programs were
distributed. The square dances were as popular as the
waltzes, schottisches, and polkas. Antone Thurman was
generally floor manager. In late years Jim Borland was
the official caller, and made a good job of it. To be a
good dancer was, in those days, considered one of the
highest forms of accomplishment. At midnight an
elaborate supper was served at one or two of the hotels,

Shift coming from work in Standard mine

Part of one side of Main Street of Bodie when town was rebuilt after fire of 1892

where the tables were laden with all the delicacies of the season.

Thus did Bodie carry out the tradition of the "Gay 90's."

The Fourth of July celebrations were something long to be remembered. All the buildings were decorated with flags and bunting. The "Daily Press" ran a two column ad, listing the events of the day. The "Grand Parade" started at 9:30 a.m., and was three blocks long, divided into different divisions. All the lodges of the town marched in full regalia. Bands and drum corps played along the line of march. There was a "Car of State," with young girls all in white waving the banners of the different States. Several hook and ladder companies rolled along. Veterans of the Mexican and Civil wars marched. There were many more parts too numerous to mention.

The afternoon was given up to contests in all kinds of athletic sports: racing, jumping, throwing, hard rock drilling, tug-of-war between the miners, and so on. In the evening the "Grand Ball" was held at the Miners' Union Hall. The "Daily Free Press" lists 75 names of people who were appointed on the various ball committees. On the 5th and 6th of July the Cornish wrestling tournament was held in Brown's corral. (Many Cornish miners were employed in the mines.) The Fourth of July celebrations were kept up as long as Bodie had any population, and were attended by people from far and near. During later years the gala appearance of the town was enhanced by foliage: huge loads of aspen, willow and poplar trees were brought into town on large wagons and placed in front of all the buildings, even the homes.

(The elevation of Bodie is so high, 8,300 feet, that trees will not grow there.)

On July, 1892, a disastrous fire swept the main street. The fire started in a restaurant building owned by a Mrs. James Perry, at about 2 o'clock in the morning. The flames leaped from building to building, and it was apparent that the west side of the street was doomed. It was but a short time before the Goodson Building and Nat Boyd's Occidental Hotel, on the east side of the street, were ablaze. All hope departed when the firemen attached the hose to the hydrant and there was no stream of water. The reservoir was full, but something had gone wrong somewhere. People were trying to fight the fire with what water they could get from pumps and wells, but to no avail; the relentless flames were devouring everything in their path.

Day dawned upon a scene of desolation. Where once had stood prosperous business houses nothing remained but ruins; not an eating house, not a lodging house was left. The residential section was untouched, and people opened their homes to those who had been burned out. The Miners' Union Hall, Boone's Brick Store, the Land Office Building, and several others on the upper block had not burned, and the fire had been halted at the bank building, as by that time the water mains were working. But little of Main Street was left, and only $3,500 in insurance had been carried, while the loss ran into hundreds of thousands of dollars.

After people had recovered from the first shock they began to think about rebuilding, which they did. Many buildings were brought from the back streets to replace those that had burned, but Bodie had shrunken perceptibly.

ADVENT OF ELECTRIC POWER

Up to this time all the hoists and mills in the camp had been run by steam power, an expensive and laborious way. Electric power had been developed, but was used only at the source of development.

Tom Legett, the Superintendent of the Standard Mine, was of the opinion that electricity could be transmitted over wires from a distance. After many meetings and discussions, the company finally agreed to act on his advice and build an electric plant thirteen miles away, at Green Creek above Bridgeport. Here a power site was located. The Standard bought the land they needed from the land and cattle baron of Mono County, T. B. Rickey, and construction on the plant was started.

Always the doubt existed as to whether or not it would be a success. It was called "Legett's Folly." Others complained the company was throwing away the stockholders' money.

When the power line was surveyed the surveyors had instructions to make it absolutely straight, no angles, no curves, which might cause the power to jump off into space. A telephone line was built parallel to the power line. The Standard Mill was shut down and equipped with agitators, motors, generators and everything needed to change from steam to this questionable power. Again the stockholders protested at the expense and the shutdown due to this change. Tom Legett and those of the staff realized if this experiment turned out to be a failure their reputations would be ruined.

At last all was in readiness for testing the "great experiment." The engineer at Green Creek called over the telephone, "At 12 o'clock noon we turn the juice into the wires." A small crowd of very tense men

assembled in front of the switch board in the Standard
Mill. The switches on both ends were thrown in.
Slowly the lights came on, dimly at first, then brighter.
The wheels of the small motor began to turn, then the
big motors were heard to vibrate, then came the joyful
sound of a steady hum. *Yes,* electric power *could* be
transmitted for a distance over wires. A more jubilant
crowd of men could not be found anywhere. They
hugged each other, threw their hats into the air and
shouted. Then someone broke a bottle of champagne
over the first motor to turn by long distance power.

No word ever flashed around the world more quickly,
and there was a scramble for power sites from Rhodesia
to Australia.

All of these Bodie engineers were at once offered
wonderful positions by the English Government. Tom
Legett afterwards built many power plants in South
Africa.

(The Green Creek plant developed 6600 volts and 350
electrical horsepower.)

In 1895 the somewhat declining Bodie was given a
shot in the arm by the cyanide process having been
discovered. There were thousands of tons of tailings
lying around Bodie. The tailings were treated with a
solution of cyanide of potassium, the most deadly poison
known. The gold was thus put into liquid form. This
solution, carrying the liquid gold, was then run through
a series of boxes containing zinc shavings. The liquid
gold precipitated on the zinc, coming back in the form
of metal. The zinc was burned away with acid, bringing
the gold back to its original state. Nine cyanide plants
were rapidly constructed, and bullion was produced

from what had been considered a bothersome and worthless lot of fine yellow sand.

In 1899 the Standard Mill, a wooden structure, which had been built at a cost of $100,000, burned to the ground. Many millions of dollars worth of bullion had been ground out by that old mill. Lester Bell, who had worked there many years, used to tell of the times they had to close down the mill to clean out the batteries. The stamps had become so clogged with amalgam they couldn't move.

A new mill was quickly built to replace the old. It, too, was only a 20-stamp mill, but a large building went up. It was a frame structure, covered with heavy corrugated iron, and is still standing.

Around 1900, many men who afterwards became

Standard Mill

prominent in the mining world, had positions in Bodie:
Dr. Frank L. Bosqui, who came to Bodie and practiced
as an M.D., studied cyaniding there, and later became
an authority on that process. He wrote two books on
the subject. Charles Merrill, who invented the Merrill
filters, became a millionaire. Paul Milton Downing,
the electrician, who was afterwards a chief executive
of the Pacific Gas and Electric Company of San Francisco. Theodore Hoover, brother of Herbert Hoover
(the latter used to visit him there, the house still
stands). John Parr, who "cyanided" in Bodie and
afterward went to South Africa to introduce the
cyanide process in Rhodesia. John C. Bawden, who
rose from foreman to superintendent. He had the old
fills worked, found new ledges, and made a pile of
money for the company. 'Twas said, "Bawden had a
nose for ore." William H. Landers, afterwards General Manager of the New Almaden Quicksilver Mine

Hoover house

near San Jose. Many others could be mentioned who made outstanding successes.

After 1900 Bodie went along in quite a normal, and I might say, uneventful way.

In 1915 the Standard Mining Property was taken over by the J. S. Cain Company.

War I put a crimp in gold mining. Quicksilver, a must in the recovery of gold, went from $70 a flask to $225, and everything else needed in the mining industry rose in proportion. The cost of deep mining skyrocketed.

The Cain Company, a little later, built a crushing plant and cyanide plant below the Standard dumps, to work the lowgrade ores. This turned out to be a failure, as the immense amount of clay in the dumps clogged the canvas and screens of the plant and the cyanide would not work.

Then E. J. Clinton, of the Clinton Cafeterias in San Francisco, thought he had discovered a process for get-

Bodie fire of 1932

ting rid of the clay. He built a plant under the direction of Billy West of Klondike fame, but this, too, was a failure.

In 1929 the Treadwell Yukon took a lease on every property in the camp. They had O. H. Hershey, a famous mining expert, make a report on the properties. It was favorable. He recommended that they pump

Bodie Bill, age 2½ years, firebug of the Bodie fire of 1932

out the Red Cloud shaft and go down to the 900-foot level, where they would, in all probability, cut the Fortuna ledge. They went instead only to the 700-foot level, and did all their mining there. They mined about four years and then closed down. Hershey later said, had he known they were not going deeper he would not have given his recommendation.

On June 23, 1932, Bodie met with the most devastating fire in its history. It was the old story—a little boy playing with matches. It started in a vacant building back of Main Street, and in half an hour two dozen buildings were burning. In a few more hours, nearly every building of Main Street had been reduced to ashes. The same buildings that had escaped the fire of 1892 were still standing on South Main, but the fire this time had spread farther north, and the bank building had burned. Practically no insurance was carried on any of the buildings.

Klipstein-Rosecrans mill on the hill, fire of 1946

In 1935 Henry Klipstein and Jack Rosecrans, the latter representing the Spreckel's sugar interests, leased the properties of the J. S. Cain Company. A mill that cost nearly half a million dollars was built to work the lowgrade ores of the camp. World War II came on, and the operations were forced to close down. This mill lay idle until 1946, and had just started up again, with about thirty men getting things in shape, when it burned to the ground. The small insurance carried on it would not replace the crushing plant alone.

While Bodie has met with one disastrous fire after another all through its history, this is of minor consequence compared to the shutting down of the mines. If, and when, mining is again resumed the town will no doubt rise from its ashes like the fabled Phoenix, a better and more glorious Bodie.

CHAPTER FIVE

Story of Rosa May

Virgin Alley had a new sign, "The Highgrade." It swung back and forth in the breeze over the latest house of ill repute on that long street inhabited by the demimonde of the camp.

The newly arrived occupant of the Highgrade was a dark-eyed, curly headed, petite French girl by the name of Rosa May. She had lived at 18 D Street in Virginia City, and later at No. 1 Ormsby Street in Carson City, Nevada. Then Bodie beckoned with its golden, and what turned out to be, its diamond-studded hand, and Rosa answered the call.

In a short time she became the idol and toast of all the men who frequented the sporting district of the town, and they were many.

One miner was heard to remark, "She was a gal who had a smile you'd go to hell for, and never regret it." Yes, Rosa was the undisputed queen of Bodie's underworld!

It was most natural that Ernest Marks, owner and proprietor of the Laurel Palace Saloon, should fall head over heels in love with her. That was no surprise to *anyone;* but the surprise and disappointment was that Rosa seemed to have a "hankerin" after Ernest.

Ernest wasn't bad looking. He was tall and dark, with a slight mustache, and, true to the Hebrew blood in his veins, had inherited the traditional trait of making money. He lavished plenty of it on Rosa, in dia-

Rosa May

monds and furs. He allowed the other girls from the
Red Light to frequent his place at night, and dance to
the tunes that the old fiddler played, but Rosa was never
there. A shade of jealousy and rage would pass over
his face if her name was mentioned lightly by any of
his drinking customers. One evening a Cornishman
named Billy Owens, who had come into some money
on the death of his mother, called "Fire in the Head!"
and the whole house rose up for a drink. "Make it
champange, Ernest," he ordered; then, mounting a
chair, with his glass raised in his hand, he shouted:
"Here's to Rosa May, the darlingest, sweetest little
bunch of loveliness that ever came into this camp.
She's mine!" Ernest turned as white as a sheet, and,
reaching down behind the bar, he grabbed the pistol

that he had kept there for emergencies. He pointed it straight at Billy, and coolly and deliberately said, "Don't drink to that toast, Billy—or I'll fill you full of lead. No other man but *me* can toast Rosa at this bar, or any other bar in this whole damn camp." Billy was raising his glass to drink, when suddenly pistol shots sounded from behind him—and the lights went out, for some level headed customer knew Ernest meant what he said. From that time on bad blood was known to exist between Ernest and Billy.

Shortly afterwards Rosa took a trip abroad. She visited her native Paris, and flitted around Brussels and Berlin, and finally came to a standstill in Monte Carlo. Many thousands of dollars that had been lost by the miners over the round green tables of the Laurel Palace Saloon, in a Western Boom Town, were laid on the tables in the luxurious gambling halls of Monte Carlo.

Finally Rosa returned to Bodie; her coming being heralded in advance by ten or fifteen trunks, which were deposited on her porch in Virgin Alley. Yes, Rosa had come home with much finery and many jewels. She replaced the red lantern that hung on her porch with a fine hand wrought iron one with a red panel glass. She also brought silver door knobs, fine furniture and mirrors throughout the house.

During her absence the "Fortuna Ledge" had been discovered in the Standard Mine. It was almost pure gold, worth thousands of dollars a pound. The miners, most of them, didn't scruple about landing down in town with some of it sticking around in their lunch buckets. The miner's code seemed to be "Hadn't the Lord put it in the ground, and didn't it belong to anybody who found it?'' Rosa came by a fair share of the highgrade. The miners' prettiest and most glistening samples were saved for her. She bought more and more diamonds from Frank Golden—the jeweler. One day she came to Frank Golden with some of the richest and most beautiful specimens she had. ''Make me a pair of cuff links and a match box out of this highgrade, Frank,'' she said. ''Make the frames of the pure gold and face it with the quartz. On the back of the match box I want the initials E. M. engraved, and make it sentimental by engraving the touching little figure of a cupid underneath.'' This was *the proof* the miners needed that she did love Ernest Marks.

In the due course of time Ernest was presented with these tokens of Rosa's affection. He proudly displayed

Ernest Marks

them on every slightest pretext. It was strange how many cigars he always had to light in the presence of customers, and how damn anxious he was to have someone tell Billy Owens about the gifts and where he got them.

A hard, cold winter soon held the camp in its icy grip; deep snows, below zero temperatures, "pneumonia weather." Rosa went from one miner's cabin to another, nursing the men who were stricken. Many a letter she penned home—for the doomed miners—to loved ones. Many a time she closed tired eyes that would never open again. Then the day came when she found it impossible to go on her mission of mercy. She had contracted the dreaded pneumonia. In a few days she was dead. She was buried in the "Outcast Cemetery," "Boot Hill"; and Ernest had a picket fence placed around her grave. "Some day," he told himself, "Rosa would have a fitting monument," but that day never came, although she left him a fortune in money and diamonds.

But the day *did* come when the Fortuna ledge faulted, dropped somewhere, was lost. The camp was on the decline; so was the fortune of Ernest Marks. The "boom camp" became a "ghost town." A few of the old inhabitants held on, and Billy Owens and Ernest Marks were two of them. Gradually the feud of other years was somewhat healed, but not forgotten. Occasionally they played cards together to pass the time. On pleasant days they always sat outside on the bench in front of the empty, neglected gambling hall and saloon. Many times Ernest would take the gold match box from his vest pocket and light a cigar, always holdin' the side with E. M., and the touching cupid, so that

Billy could see them. Then Billy would turn his head in the opposite direction, looking in a reminiscent way into space—and would not speak for several minutes.

Rosa's fabulous jewels were being sold one by one

Rosa May's red lantern

by Ernest, all far below their real intrinsic value. Then the day came when there were no more to sell; but the match box and cuff links were still his, and a trunk full of Rosa's finery and keepsakes, that he had treasured and loved all these years.

Finally Ernest fell ill. He had a lingering illness. Billy Owens was his constant companion and his nurse. Relatives in New York were informed of his condition and circumstances. They sent him regular remittances until he died. His last request, to be buried beside Rosa, was granted. Billy Owens himself dug the grave.

Billy was downhearted and lonely after Ernest died. He lived by himself in an old ramblin' lodging house

Match box and cuff links

that belonged to his mother—"Grandma Johnston."
Only empty rooms surrounded him. Every door he
locked tight, and he barricaded himself in one little
room. One morning no smoke came from the chimney,
and when a miner broke into Billy's house he found
him dead.

Billy was badly in debt. In order to pay his debts,
and defray his funeral expenses, the Sheriff auctioned
off his lodging house and all its contents. Among other
things a trunk was brought out and sold—contents un-
seen. It contained the finery, pictures and letters of
Rosa May. Behind a family picture, in a knothole in
the wall, concealed by several layers of wall paper which
were pasted over it, was found Billy's valuables: three
gold-plated watches, a horseshoe stickpin, a picture of
his mother—in a locket, a few silver coins, and a solid
gold match box and cuff links—faced with quartz, and
initialed E. M. There was nothing much of value, ex-
cept the match box and cuff links. The bidding was
spirited on these, and brought in more than a hundred
dollars. His day of triumph had arrived. The match
box and cuff links *buried* Billy Owens.

CHAPTER SIX

Wells Fargo Messengers and Desperadoes of the Road

No history of Bodie would be complete without mention of the brave Wells Fargo messengers who guarded the strong boxes, containing millions in gold bullion, that were shipped out of Bodie on the stage lines.

The messengers always sat on the front seat of the stage to the left of the driver, gun in hand, peering into the darkness for those wealth crazed bandits who would rather get rich by robbing than by working. It was a game of life or death on both sides, and the result depended on which one was the quicker on the draw. Often, if the shipment warranted it, there were two messengers, one sitting in front, the other in back.

The most noted of the Wells Fargo messengers who came to Bodie were Aaron Ross, Oliver Roberts, Mike Tovey, Alex Montgomery, Eugene Blair, and Alex Burke. Their life histories and experiences would make and fill a most interesting book. They were all men of fine physique, tall and straight as a mountain pine.

Aaron Ross had been nicknamed "Lost Charlie," on account of his family name being the same as the kid-

napped "Lost Charlie Ross" of Philadelphia. Before
coming to Bodie he had been a messenger out of Elko,
Nevada, and in an encounter with train robbers en route
to Ogden he had, single handed, killed two and wounded
three; he himself coming out without a scratch. "Watch
the ears of the pointer team," Lost Charlie used to say.
"A horse can scent danger quicker than a human, and
he tells you about it with his ears. He holds them erect,
with quick little jerks backwards, and when you see
this danger signal, get the butt of your gun to your
shoulder and get the trigger cocked for business, as
only the fraction of a second may stand between you
and death."

When the United States Government contracted,
during World I, to move $32,000,000 in gold and silver
from San Francisco to Denver, Colorado, they selected
Aaron Ross, although he was getting old, as a shotgun
messenger to guard this enormous shipment. During
all his years of service with Wells Fargo he had had a
clean record, never having lost a shipment of bullion,
though he had numerous encounters with the most desperate bandits of his time. It was told that he had
killed or wounded at least a score of them, coming out
of these desperate fights with only minor wounds.

"Lost Charlie" Ross was later made an investigator
of robberies by Wells Fargo. He had taken Oliver
Roberts in tow as likely timber to succeed him as messenger, and he was correct in his choice. Roberts proved
himself to be as fearless a man as ever guarded a Wells
Fargo box.

At times the bullion was concealed in other places
than the locked and bolted strong box. It might be in
the center of a roll of dirty bedding, or a battered suit-

case, whereas the Wells Fargo box contained lead molds. But this was the exception rather than the rule.

Mike Tovey was shot on the Bodie road at one time, when he had a rather unknown messenger by the name of Woodruff sent to help him guard the treasure. The morning stage had been held up and robbed, and Tovey, going down on a later stage, decided to get out and walk ahead of the stage near the place of the earlier holdup. As he approached, the robbers opened fire. Tovey shot and killed one, while robber No. 2 fired and shot Tovey in the arm, and then killed the leader horse on the stage. Tovey was taken to a near-by cabin, and given first aid. Woodruff was left to guard the box. His story was that robber No. 2 came back and made his getaway with the treasure. That he, Woodruff, had failed to kill or wound him because the gun he was using was crooked. Aaron Ross was sent by Wells Fargo to investigate the holdup. He reported that, upon examination, he found it was the *man* and not the *gun* that was crooked.

The dead thief, killed by Tovey, had effects on his person that identified him as Frank Jones of San Francisco, and his roommate and accomplice as one Charles Sharp, a notorious bandit of that time.

Sharp was later apprehended as he was entering the room that he and Jones had shared in San Francisco. He was brought back and lodged in jail in Aurora, Nevada, as this was the nearest town to where the holdup had taken place. Sharp immediately proceeded to plan his escape. This he made in a short time, by hollowing out the mortar in a brick wall with a jack-knife.

Aaron Ross again took up the search, which led him to Southern California, where Sharp was apprehended.

He was later convicted, and was sentenced to several years in the Carson Prison.

The bandits most feared in this part of the country were the Small and McDonald gang; Vascus and Chavis, dreaded Mexican outlaws, and the lone workers, "Three Fingered Jack" and "Johnny Behind the Rocks."

"Johnny Behind the Rocks" had figured out a plan in his warped brain that if he could throw large enough boulders down on the stage from some narrow canyon ledge he could cause the horses to run away, thereby upsetting the stage and making it possible for him to obtain the loot. He tried this at different times, without success.

Eugene Blair had several encounters with robbers, but successfully protected his strong box against them, although he suffered on two occasions from serious wounds.

Numerous messengers had met their deaths before Charlie Ross came upon the scene, but his draw had been so quick and his aim so sure in his messenger days, and his sleuthing so dogged and determined in his detective days, that he somewhat brought to a halt these desperadoes.

Messenger Alex Burke was tipped off one time to an intended holdup. An underworld character claimed to have received this information from a woman in the Red Light District. The stage was to be held up next morning, about nine miles down from Bodie near a narrow pass called Devils Gate. The plan was to stretch a tense wire from one canyon wall to the other, so that the horses would be tripped at about their knees. The stage generally passed this point just about daylight.

Burke had the driver postpone the trip until around 8 o'clock. Whether the bandits got wise on account of the delay in stage time was not known, but the holdup did not take place. However, it was said that a long piece of cable had been found near the spot, with two large iron stakes that had been uprooted from opposite places across the road and thrown into a ditch.

Alex Burke spent the last years of his life in Yerington, Nevada, where he died. One of his granddaughters married a grandson of Jim Cain.

Early in 1880, on the old stage road from Bodie to Carson, two Mexican bandits took $30,000 in bullion off the stage. The Sheriff and his posse picked up their trail the following day, killed one bandit and buried him on the spot. His confederate was taken alive, and he either committed suicide or was smothered to death in his cell, as he was found dead the next morning.

Wells Fargo offered a reward for the return of the bullion. A champion driller of Nevada named McCullough, and Frank Holmes, a miner, hunted for months for the cache, but it was never found.

In later years a holdup was staged in the melting room at the Standard Mill. That beat anything for daring that was ever pulled off in, or around, Bodie. The bullion was in molten form, ready to be poured in the molds, when the assayer who was doing the melting decided to go to supper. A tough who had been watching, and knew his habits, came up over the hill on which the melting room was located. As soon as the assayer left he took up the job where the melter had left off, poured the sizzling red hot molten bullion into the molds, turned the cold water on them from a hose, and proceeded to carry them one by one down the steep hill.

He had dug a hole in which to bury them, in the tailings pond, farther down at the foot of the hill. Had he not returned for the very last, and smallest of the molds, he would in all probability have successfully carried out the robbery, and perhaps never even been suspicioned.

Joe Beck, the watchman employed by the Standard Company for a lifetime, showed up on the scene just as the robber was coming out of the assay office for the last time. They exchanged shots and both were wounded, neither fatally. The fellow gave himself up, as, being unmasked, Joe Beck knew who he was. He pleaded guilty in the Justice Court and was given a chance to leave town. Bodie was not too hard on those who tried to get their share of the yellow metal, of which there seemed to be so much. It had been introduced to just another form of highgrading.

In 1914 the Bodie Bank was robbed, supposedly by a gang of four bad characters from Yerington, Nevada. They left their automobile parked down the road about a mile from town and walked up to the bank. They used an electric drill to gain entrance into the vault. Inside the vault was a large two compartment safe. One side was open and contained about $4,000 in money and jewelry. This they put into sacks which they carried. They were not able to get into the other side of the safe, being frightened away by people who had attended a dance and were passing the bank in the early morning hours. What they really had come for, and expected to get, was a bar of bullion worth about $10,000, which had been shipped out on the stage the morning before. They were tracked into Nevada, and at Rawhide some fragments of the jewelry were found in an old blacksmith's forge, where they had melted it up. It was said at the time that not too much effort was put into the attempt to apprehend them, as it was supposed they had well known family connections.

The old time bandits and stage robbers are no more. They are as much a part of the romantic gold rush days as were the pioneers, the gold seekers, and the gamblers. They had their place in the kaleidoscope of color and enchantment that formed the picture of

> "The Days of Old,
> The Days of Gold,
> The Days of '49."

CHAPTER SEVEN

Story of Jim Cain

(Editor's note: It seems strange that I have been searching through newspapers and books to learn what has been written about J. S. Cain, my father-in-law, with whom I had lived in close contact for over thirty years. Sometimes we are so close to a mountain that we fail to get the true perspective, like those who view it from a distance. It is not amiss that I should compare Jim Cain to a mountain, which has basked in the warmth of sunshine, and has also known the storm clouds gather and the tempest burst around its head in fury. In his later years he manfully withstood the shocks, always having faith that on a bright tomorrow the sun would shine once more in a rosy glow over his beloved Bodie.)

James Stuart Cain was born in Rockburn, Province of Quebec, Canada, in 1854. His parents were farmers, and exported maple sugar and maple syrup to the United States. Chateaugay, New York, is just across the border from Rockburn.

At 21 years of age Jim answered the cry of the Far West, coming to Carson City, Nevada.

He was light complexioned, tall, straight, and ambitious; always a hard worker by day and a thinker by night. He was sociable, had a keen sense of humor, and liked nothing better than to play practical jokes on his friends. All through his life he was an optimist. When things went wrong in his later years he was worried, but was never heard to complain. He would always say, "It's not too serious."

His first job was in a lumber yard in Carson Valley. It was located at the foot of a flume that brought the lumber from Glenbrook, Lake Tahoe. This lumber was being used in the mines at Virginia City. After a time he became foreman of the V & T Railroad in Carson City. During the time he was working in Carson City he met and married Martha Delilah Wells ("Lile" he always called her), who was living in Genoa, the first settlement in Nevada. She was born at Willow Creek, Utah, and her uncle was Governor Wells of that State.

When the gold excitement was at its height in Bodie, Jim and Lile decided to cast their lot in the then booming camp, going there in 1879. Jim's first job was with the Porter Lumber Company, and they lived in a house, which is still standing, opposite the Methodist Church.

In 1880 Lile went to Carson City, Nevada, for the birth of their first child, David Victor. Lile had made all of David Victor's baby clothes in the house opposite the Methodist Church. (Years later David Victor's own three children were born in this same house.) Three other children were born to Jim and Lile; they were Jessie D., James II, and Stuart Wells.

When Jim had saved enough money he put lumber barges on Mono Lake, to bring the lumber from Mono Mills across the lake. Later he and Thomas Holt leased the Bodie Railroad and lumber yard.

He had a friend named Joe Maguire, an old Irishman

James Stuart Cain

from Virginia City. They decided to take a lease on the
block of ground in the Standard Mine, struck a fabu-
lously rich ledge, and took out $90,000 in 90 days. Joe,
being Irish, and therefore superstitious, attributed all
their luck to the fact that he had refused to sign the
lease on Friday. From then on everything seemed to
come Jim Cain's way. He bought the Bodie Bank from
E. L. Benedict in 1890, and started investing his money
in different lines of business around town. Having a
passionate love of horses, and realizing Bodie needed
some kind of outdoor recreation, he formed the Bodie

Lile Wells Cain

Race Track Association, with other business men, and an up-to-date race track was built at Booker Flat.

His favorite trotting horse, which won many races, was Bodie Bird.

Bodie went wild over horse racing. Mike Tulley, a gambler, went on the outside and brought in horses to beat the local ones. The betting was spirited, and they sent the gambler, with his pockets flat, back to Nevada.

Many a laugh was caused by the jokes J. S. played on his friends.

At one time, while in San Francisco, he conspired with two of his friends to play a joke on a third. The three men were to make a trip to Bodie shortly, via the Sonora road. J. S. was to station two masked men, pre-

Bodie Bird, Jim Cain's race horse

sumably bandits, to hold up the party at a narrow place on the grade. The "bandits" were to take whatever money was in the pockets of the two taller men, who knew the plans, and from the stout man they were to take only a very valuable gold watch attached to a nugget chain, which he wore conspicuously across his vest. The "holdup" came off without a hitch, and J. S.'s friends arrived in Bodie in a highly excitable state, the two men who were on to the joke playing their parts exceedingly well. The stout man kept lamenting the fact that his watch and chain were taken instead of his cash, which was apparently overlooked. On going to San Francisco he gave the daily papers an account of the "holdup," which they published, along with the description of his stolen watch and chain. J. S. and the others realized the joke had gone a little too far by that time, but they could not possibly tell A. and make an enemy of him forever. J. S. had the watch in his safe for nearly two years. Then he shipped it back to A. from Reno, Nevada, enclosing a note from the "bandit," saying his conscience had bothered him so much that he had decided to return the watch, knowing to whom it had belonged by the piece he had cut out of the paper. Several days later J. S. received the following telegram: "My watch was returned to me by a penitent thief. Will write particulars later. Signed A——."

(Editor's note: If A. is still alive I hope he will not read this.)

It was known that a mining man by the name of Warren Loose took a certain lady, whom he was courting, for a sleigh ride every Sunday afternoon. It was his habit to park the sleigh in front of Burkham's store,

go into the store and buy a bottle of wine, then take
the wine out and put it in the seat of the sleigh under
the robes. He would then go into the local barber shop
to get "prettied up." J. S. watched his chance, stole
the bottle, and replaced the wine with water. The next
day Warren confided to J. S. what had happened on
his ride. "Why, you know, J. S., there was nothing
but water in that bottle. Alma drank first, and didn't
say a word, but when I drank you could have knocked
me over with a toothpick—I felt so cheap. Do you
suppose that old 'so and so' of a Burkham is selling
water for wine?"

A little Chinaman, dubbed "Chickie," used to go into
the bank to phone, after having been convinced the telephone would talk Chinese as well as English. He used
to call the Wells Fargo agent in Hawthorne to find out
if his produce was there, and to ask him to get it on

Viewing the races from autos about 1900 before the grand stand
at the race track was built

the next stage. He invariably asked about sweet potatoes. J. S. put three sweet potatoes in the battery box
of the old fashioned telephone. Then he put the Wells
Fargo agent in Hawthorne wise. The next time Chickie
phoned Hawthorne the agent said, "I'll send the sweet
potatoes up by wire—right now." Chickie turned to
J. S. "He said sweet potatoes come right now," whereupon J. S. opened the phone box and out rolled the sweet
potatoes onto the floor. The Chink dropped the receiver
in amazement, then grabbed it up again and hollered
into the phone: "Holy gee! These come velly damn
quick—Send *everything."*

Jim had bought the Bodie stables and freight teams
from Harvey Boone. The freighting in those days paid
a handsome profit, but required keeping about a hundred head of horses. Jim loved nothing better than a
good horse trade. If he got the best of the other fellow
in a horse trade he would subsequently let him know
about it, and laugh long and heartily.

He was affiliated with the Masons, and was Past
Master of that order.

The Bodie Bank escaped the fire of 1892. "Jim Cain's
luck," they said.

A few months later long distance power was transmitted from Green Creek to Bodie; the first long distance power plant in the world. Jim was one of the
few big stockholders in the Standard Mine who was in
favor of building this plant, to test if electricity could
be transmitted a long distance over wires. He counted
it one of the biggest thrills in his life when the wheels
in the Standard Mill began to turn.

When the cyanide process was discovered J. S. Cain
and A. J. McCone, a prominent mining and foundry

man of Virginia City, Nevada, located and bought
nearly all the tailings in and around Bodie. They hired
an expert from New Zealand, who was familiar with
the process, to build the first plant and work the tailings. His salary was $1,000 a month and found, which
included a horse and buggy for his use. This was an
unheard of salary in those days, but Cain and McCone
figured he was worth it. They built the South End

Bodie bank

plant, the biggest plant in the United States at that time. Under this expert, J. S. put in, as his assistant, his brother-in-law, Lester E. Bell. When Lester learned the process he took charge of the plant. "Honest Old Lester," he was always called, and 'twas said no matter how much gold passed through his hands none of it ever stuck to his fingers. Three other plants were built in quick succession by Cain and McCone: the Bodie Tunnel Plant, the Victor, and the Del Monte.

The farmers down the canyon and on into Nevada, who were supplied with water from Bodie Creek, had *previously* put an injunction on the Bodie mines, prohibiting them from letting any more tailings wash into the creek. The tailings had deposited a yellow coat of soil over their farming lands. Thereafter the tailings, with their golden treasure, had to be banked up in Bodie. Little did the farmers dream that by this injunction they were stopping a golden flood from pouring over their land, nor little did they dream of the profit they would realize from the yellow coat which had *already* been deposited. Sometime later Cain and McCone sent their cyanide men down to help the farmers build plants on their own ranches (a small plant was not costly) and they worked the tailings for themselves. After the tailings were worked crops were again planted, but this time there wasn't any "gold from the grass roots up."

Bodie drifted on at a quiet and even keel during the rest of the '90's. Cain and McCone were mining in the Bodie. They had run a tunnel for some distance and hadn't struck a ledge. The Standard, however, offered them $50,000 for the claim, which they took. A few months afterwards the Standard cross-cut the Bodie and took out $7,000,000. At that time Alec McCone wanted J. S. Cain to invest the money they received from the Bodie in a business in San Francisco. Cain said, "Alec, you take San Francisco, I'll stick with Bodie." Alec McCone went into the machinery business in San Francisco, in the well known firm of Harron, Ricard & McCone. His son, John A. McCone, is now a millionaire of Los Angeles, California.

Later Harry Gorham, Senator Jim Woodbury, and Alec McCone, all of Nevada, sold out the Aurora mines to Jesse Knight of Utah at a handsome figure. Harry Gorham had his eye on the then vacant tract of land where Santa Monica now stands. "Come with me, Jim," pleaded Harry Gorham, "the South is the coming place." "No thanks," again answered Jim Cain. Harry Gorham did buy the Santa Monica tract, subdivided it, established the Bank of Santa Monica, and made a fortune.

After the Green Creek plant had been built Jim Cain located other power sites in Mono County: the Leevining site, at the head of Silvester Meadows, and the Rush Creek site, at Silver Lake. He realized here was potential power for the cities to the south, and, sooner or later, they would need them. Holding these power sites was a big expense, as the law required that work developing them had to be done continuously. When ranches controlling water rights were for sale in Mono Basin Jim bought them. He finally got a worthwhile offer for his holdings from the Pacific Power Company, now the California Electric Power Co., receiving as part consideration a large block of stock in the new company. The stock that went on the boards at $4.00 a common share, reached $125.00 in a few years.

Still J. S. Cain's one thought and interest was in mining. He had cherished a secret dream in his heart that if he ever was able to own or control the Standard Mine he would again find the gold-laden Fortuna vein, which had faulted. It was a large, strong ledge when it suddenly dropped from sight. Geologists differed in their opinions as to where it might be picked up again. Jim Cain had an idea, and some day he might be able to prove it.

The years from 1900 to 1915 passed along in quite an even keel. The mines of the camp were sending out regular shipments of bullion. J. S. Cain owned and operated a claim adjoining the Standard, called the Midnight. One day the miners in the Midnight, following along a good ledge, suddenly broke into a workings they had not dug and did not know existed. The Standard had been taking out ore from the Midnight. Litigation ensued. Cain hired, as his attorney, his old friend Billy Metson of San Francisco. It was a lengthy trial with scores of witnesses on both sides. When a former Superintendent of the Standard testified, under oath, that under his orders and with the consent of the Standard management the ore had been deliberately and fraudulently taken out of the Midnight, the case was practically won for J. S. Cain. Big damages were awarded the Midnight, but a compromise was made by the warring parties and Cain took over the Standard property.

The bright star under which J. S. Cain seemed to have been living suddenly reached its zenith. Thousands of dollars were spent in search of the Fortuna ledge. Jim Cain could have said with Robert Service:

STORY OF JIM CAIN   87

> "There's gold and it's haunting and haunting
> It's luring me on as of old
> Yet it isn't the gold that I'm wanting
> So much as just finding the gold."

and it might be added, "but, dear Lord, let it be in the Fortuna ledge." What Jim Cain had been *dreaming* of, had been *striving* for, was recapturing the great thrill he had known when he and Joe Maguire had struck that then unknown ledge, in the early days; but it wasn't to be. His gold was poured back almost as rapidly as it had come out, but the lost Fortuna was never found. Later the Standard Mine was thrown open to leasers, with more or less success.

Then Jim met with another and another disappointment. He built a cyanide plant in Lundy (they had always been a success) but this one turned out to be a failure. The tailings which had been run into Lundy Lake were pumped out. They had become mixed with sawdust that had run into the lake, and the values could not be extracted. A second plant, built to work low grade ores near the Standard dumps, was also a failure.

Lile's health failed in the early '20's, and she left the high altitude to live in San Francisco with her daughter and son-in-law, Dolly and Emil Billeb, and their children.

After Lile went away Jim's son Victor and his family lived with him in the old Cain home in Bodie.

In 1936 Lile and Jim's son, James II, died in San Francisco.

In World War II six of Jim and Lile's eight grandsons, two of them commissioned officers, fought for their county on far-flung battlefields all over the world.

The Cains still own Bodie, and still believe it has a future. It is well guarded by the faithful watchman, Martin Gianettoni.

Dolly (Mrs. Billeb) lives in San Francisco. The two Cain sons, Victor and Stuart, have businesses in Bridgeport, within sight of Potato Peak and Mount Biddleman, which stand like sentinels guarding their old home town.

Some day, in the near future, will there be a sequel to this story, telling that the faith J. S. Cain had in Bodie was justified?

CHAPTER EIGHT

Jim Pender's Stories of Lundy

Now for some stories of Lundy. Case you don't know where Lundy is, it's another old minin' camp in the Sierra Nevada Mountains, 'bout six miles northwest o' Mono Lake, an' twenty miles from Bodie.

When God put gold in Lundy canyon He put it in the prettiest and choicest spot old Mother Nature had to offer; lofty peaks a touchin' the sky, deep gorges, waterfalls, streams all bordered with quakin' asp and Jeffrey pines, and a lake that nestled like a gem 'atween the mountains, and reflected on her bosom all the beauties of nature.

Around 1878 W. J. Lundy had started operatin' a sawmill on the lake named for him. He was supplyin' Bodie with lumber, as that town was havin' a hell roarin' boom 'bout that time.

Some prospectors named W. D. Wasson, C. H. Nye and L. L. Homer began prospectin' around these parts and came upon some good croppin's of ore. They sent over to Bodie for J. G. McClinton, him bein' the authority on minin', an' also the best promoter around

the country. McClinton was impressed by the showin'
they had, so together they organized the Homer Minin'
District of Mono County, but the little settlement was
called Lundy.

Town of Lundy

Homer, in whose honor the district was named, killed himself in San Francisco. Some said his suicide was caused by financial worries; some said it was family trouble. I reckon it was a little of both, for the people of Lundy sort of sat up an' took notice when his estate was settled, to find the woman they had knowed as Mrs. Homer was in reality a Hattie C. Aitkins.

Well, it wasn't long afore all kinds of claims were bein' staked out in the Homer District: the Nioma, Bonanza, Savage, Grand Prize, Last Chance, an' many others. The one that really turned out to be a mine was the May Lundy, with a production of $2,000,000. It was situated like an eagle's nest on the top of the mountain 'bove the town. Lordy God! that mountain was so steep hardly a squirrel could climb it. Course there was a

The main street of Lundy, looking south

gold rush to the new camp, an' boardin' houses, saloons, stores, dwellin' houses, an' China Town, seemed to be built over night. The settin' was so pretty, there in th' heart o' nature, that it seemed this must have been the one exception to the miners' theory, that "Where God puts gold He doesn't put anything else."

The leadin' merchandise store was owned by a fine man named Butterfield, an' the Lundy Hotel was run by a Mrs. Al Taylor. Jack Murray an' George Fry owned th' two principal saloons. Into these saloons the miners crowded 'till there wasn't even standin' room, an' the gang would paint that pretty little town as red as hell every payday. Why, the decent element couldn't sleep at night when the boys had cashed their

May Lundy mine

pay checks an' got goin'. You'll hear more of Murray's
and Fry's saloons as I get along with my stories.

I'm thirsty, now, Mister. Will you buy me a drink?

There was an Irish character named Bill Monahan
drifted in here from Bodie. 'Twas sort of whispered
around that he'd been run out of there 'count of his
part in the holdin' up of a stable man. Bill was a
happy-go-lucky sort, but he had one fault. He was always a braggin' about what a brave man he was, an'
how "Bill Monahan wouldn't take water from anny
body." The boys had their doubts 'bout Bill's courage,
but they didn't have no way to prove it.

Now there had been a Chinaman's grave dug up a
little south of the cemetery, an' his bones shipped back

Boarding house and bunks at May Lundy mine

to China, seein' as how he would rest better there. Bill used to pasture his horse on the patch of grass below the cemetery, and as the path ran along side of this yawnin' grave, Bill went by it every night. One day there was a bunch of the boys celebratin' in Murray's saloon, an' they got to figurin' as to how they could test Bill's courage. Chuck, whose brain was a workin' a little better than th' others, thought of a scheme. He'd wind himself up in a sheet an' crawl into the Chinaman's empty grave, and when Bill passed he'd raise up an' scare hell out of him. "Say! he'll come into this saloon whiter than the snow on Mt. Gilcrest."

They laughed and they drank, and they drank and they laughed, thinkin' of the fun they was a goin' to have with Bill.

That night, 'bout the usual time, Bill tethered Pete down in the pasture, swung the halter over his shoulder an' started back to town. He was singin' an old Irish "Come all ye" as he neared the spot where Chuck was crouchin' down in the hole. Lordy God! When Chuck sprang up an' waved his sheet around in a menacin' way, Bill just grabbed the halter off his shoulder an' started landin' on him. "Get back in your hole—you yellow skin Son of a B," and to save himself from bein' killed Chuck had to jump back—with his head a bleedin' all over that white sheet.

When Bill got back to Murray's Saloon the boys were a waitin'. "What do you think, boys?" says Bill, "they wouldn't have that old dead Chink in China an' he's landed back here again." "Shure an' I put him in his place with my halter." There was dead silence, with the boys just standin' lookin' at each other; then the bartender yelled, "The drinks are on the house!"

There was an editor in Lundy at this time by the name of Jim Townsend. His paper was called the "Homer Miner Index." Later he went to Bodie, an' edited the "Bodie Miner Index." Jim Townsend was a sure enough wit. It was always told in these here parts that Mark Twain and Bret Harte got a lot of their sayin's that made them famous from Jim Townsend. When th' paper came out folks all knew they was in for a laugh. Old Jim didn't spare no one's feelin's in order to get that laugh over, either; for instance, here are a few of his quips:

I.

"People should never be judged by appearances, for a shabby old coat may contain an editor, while a man wearing a high toned plug hat may be a delinquent subscriber."

II.

"A Bodie woman wants $1,000 for being kissed by Kilgore, the butcher. She says the crime was committed in the presence of 'naked calves,' 'decollette sheep,' and 'Kansas City hams in yellow tights'."

III.

"A local man was buried last week. 'Tis said before he died his good wife sorrowfully and affectionately asked him—'Don't you think you could eat a bit of something, John?' With a wan smile he said: 'I do think I could eat a bit of the ham I smelled cooking.' 'Oh, no! John, dear,' said his wife, 'you can't eat that; that's for the wake'."

IV.

"All the people who play the fiddle look something alike. Now there's J.M.C. and C.W.S."

V.

"The old time bustle has come to the front again, so that a slim woman may deceive man as to her physical condition.

VI.

"Marks has a lot of summit stock which he offers for sale: at *his own* price."

VII.

"Old Jim went around with an ear phone, and always managed to never hear anything that didn't conveniently suit him."

*   *   *   *

JIM PENDER'S STORY OF THE "CHINK" GIRL

There were some bad characters in Lundy at this time. Kirk Steve and Charlie Jardine were two of them, and they were mortal enemies—sworn to get each other's scalps. They were both known as bein' two gun men, an' each was tryin' to get the drop on the other. Kirk Steve wore a constable's badge. How he got the license to wear it no one ever knowed, but it sort o' gave him the upper hand over Charlie Jardine, case they got in a shootin' scrape—an' Jardine got blasted. Jardine got himself a "side kick" by the name of Tex Wilson, an' these two sort o' hung together, keepin' track o' what Kirk Steve was doin'.

Now there was a China girl in town by the name of Ling Loi, who had been down in th' Chinese joints all summer, an' had made herself a lot o' money. It had been noised around, by the grapevine, that Ling Loi was goin' out on the stage in a couple o' days, takin' all her wad with her. Now, Jardine had a losin' streak at poker for awhile, an' just about this time he found

himself dead broke. He'd never been given to doin'
hard work to get money, so he hit upon a plan. He
propositions Tex on holdin' up the stage, takin' the
Chink girl off, an' holdin' her for ransom. Course he'd
relieve her of the wad she had on her right away. Tex
was not only agreeable, fact is, he was plum delighted
with the whole idea. To stage a holdup would be excitin'
enough, but to steal an' make his getaway with a pretty
little gal like Ling Loi, that was somethin' that had
adventure in it.

Well, next mornin', afore daylight, Tex rode down
the canyon on horseback a few miles to where a big
bluff of rocks stood near the road. He hid himself behind it and waited for the stage to come along. Now
there was a young kid a drivin' the stagecoach who was
known by the nickname of "Curley." Curley was used
to doin' what he was told to do, so when Tex, all masked
an' with two big six shooters, jumps into the middle
of th' road, and calls "Halt!" "Hands up!" the kid
followed orders. Tex moves along, cautious like, up to
the passengers—who were stiff with fright. "I don't
mean to do you no harm," said Tex, "all I want is for
you there, the Chink girl I mean, to get down out of the
stagecoach without any fuss. Hear me?" Now Ling Loi
was a tremblin' so much she couldn't hardly move, but
when the other passengers jumped up from their seats
to give her room, she knew the only thing for her to do
was to get out. She stepped down, best she could, still
shakin' all over. Tex took her, rough-like, by the arm,
an' pulled her off to the side of the road. "That's all."
"Move on," he said, and Curley gave the horses such
a lick they plunged ahead, throwin' all th' passengers
to th' bottom of th' stage. With that Tex fired twice

into the air, to let Curley know he meant business, an'
the stage whirled away in such a cloud o' dust you
couldn't see 'em leavin'. Tex and th' Chink girl were
standin' there lookin' at each other, an' Tex took note
as to how she was a pretty lightly gal; but his worry
was to get her away afore anyone else showed up.

He took Ling Loi way up to a lonely cabin in the
mountains, that he and Jardine had decided upon.
When Jardine showed up durin' th' night, with a bottle
of whiskey and some grub, Tex had a sad story to tell
him. Some smart Chink had talked Ling Loi into
sendin' her money out by express, 'stead o' takin' it
with her. Result was she had only enough money on her
to get to San Francisco, less than $100. Then Jardine
tells Tex as to how the whole bloomin' camp is in an
uproar over the kidnappin' of Ling Loi, and how they
are threatenin' to string the guilty ones up to a telegraph pole, soon as they are found. Well, here they
were in a pretty boat, with a Chink girl without any
money to take care of, way up in the mountains, and
an angry mob threatenin' to string 'em up down in
town. Well, Tex insisted on Jardine goin' on with his
part of the agreement to get the ransom money, seein'
as how he, Tex, had carried out what he was supposed
to do.

Jardine found out, when he tried the ransom game on
the Chinks, they was not much for payin' the $2,000
to get Ling Loi back. Fact was, two other Chinese girls
had come to camp—an' were all the rage.

'Bout this time Kirk Steve an' his gang began to get
suspicious concernin' the ransom, an' agreed that Jardine knew more about the kidnappin' than he was tellin'. They hired a fellow to follow him, an' Jardine

didn't dare go up to the cabin where Tex an' Ling Loi were a hidin'. They were gettin' powerful short on food, too. Finally Tex decided they couldn't live on love any more, an' he didn't want to starve, or let pretty Ling Loi starve either, so the only thing for them to do was to get out. He put the girl behind him on the horse, and together they rode down the mountain—to the same rock where Tex had held up the stage. He sort of felt lonesome when Ling Loi headed, on foot, for Lundy, and he headed his horse in the opposite direction toward Mono Lake.

Ling Loi got into town towards midnight. There was a big gang drinkin' in George Fry's saloon. Spike

Lonely cabins on Lundy Mountains

Thomas, Kirk Steve, and Bill Callahan were full o' whiskey, and were tellin' what they would do when they caught up with Charlie Jardine an' Tex Wilson. Just at this point a Chink ran into the saloon, tellin' them that Ling Loi was back, who had kidnapped her, an' all about it. Course the Kirk Steve gang had to make good their braggin', an' they started right out on horseback after Tex Wilson. There had been a slight fall o' snow, so when they reached the big rock it wasn't hard to track Tex. When they came upon him, he was sleepin' peaceful like with his blanket wrapped around him, layin' in a dry wash down near Mono Lake. They got the drop on him.

They brought Tex back to Lundy, his arms tied fast to his sides with a lariat. Kirk Steve came first, leadin' Tex's horse, with Callahan an' Spike Thomas bringing' up the rear on horseback. They had their guns out an' leveled at Tex's back. They put Tex back of the bar in George Fry's saloon, an' one minute they voted to hang him, an' the next minute to let the law take its course. They was still votin', pro and con, when Deputy Sheriff Wilcox, who had been sent for by the decent element in Lundy, landed from Bridgeport, with six sworn-in deputies. Sheriff Kinney had anticipated trouble from the Lundy gang, an' had sent men enough to cope with the situation.

When Kirk Steve saw the Sheriff leavin' with Tex his blood was a boilin'. He was thinkin' that Tex had only been a tool for Jardine anyway, and had gotten caught, so he made up his mind to fill Jardine full of holes then and there. He met Jardine just outside the saloon, and, Lordy God, the shootin' started. Kirk had come around the corner, sort o' reelin' from drink and temper, an' Jardine up an' shot him in the stomach. With that Jardine ran into the saloon, but Kirk pulled himself up, although the blood was a runnin' into his shoes, an' he followed Jardine. His aim was true this time, an' Jardine dropped in a heap on the saloon floor. The local doctor was called, an' he pulled 'em both through; though the town would have been better off without 'em.

They didn't prefer charges against each other, knowin' they would both be sent to prison, but their henchmen on each side took up the feud. Joe Lee, a bartender in Jack Murray's saloon, was a great admirer of Jardine. He kept spoutin' off his mouth as to how Kirk Steve should have been strung up long ago, and his hide an' tallow given to the coyotes. Callahan, Kirk's "side-kick," was drinkin' in front of the bar one night an' gettin' tired of Joe Lee's tirade against Kirk Steve. He up an' hit Lee square in the face, with the butt end of his gun. Lee staggered for a minute, with the blood from his nose squirtin' all over the place, but he managed to reach down and get his gun from under the bar, where he always kept it. He shot Callahan square in the abdomen, an' he dropped to the floor like a stuck pig. There was a free-for-all fight, with guns poppin' every place, until some far-sighted miner shot the lights out.

Well, Joe Lee joined his friend Tex Wilson in the County Jail at Bridgeport the next day, and they sort o' settled down to a hum-drum life, waitin' to see what the law was a goin' to do to them. There was a Chinese in jail with 'em, waitin' to be tried for the murder of another Chink up in Bodie. When he heard what Tex was a servin' time for, he didn't talk to 'em much. Lordy

God! One day the jail door opened an' there was their friend, Charlie Jardine, with handcuffs on, bein' escorted in by Sheriff Kinney—to stand trial for his part in th' kidnappin, now that he had recovered from the gunshot wound.

Now the Sheriff's house in Bridgeport is built smack up against the jail, fact is, one wall of the jail forms the side of the Sheriff's house, an' there is a slide in this stone wall through which the meals are passed in to the prisoners.

Sheriff Kinney had a lightly daughter name of Cora, who played the pianner. Joe and Tex and Jardine used to listen, 'cause they had nothin' else to do, an' they finally got to plottin' again.

Cora used to pass the meals in to them sometimes, and Jardine would get up by the slide an' talk to her. He always was a praisin' her playin', an' askin' her to play the tunes his mother used to like. Then finally he took to singin' the songs as she played 'em on the pianner. Well, Cora was young enough to be flattered that a hard, tough character of Jardine's caliber would like her music, so she banged as loud as she could on her side of the wall, and Jardine bellowed as loud as he could on the other side. All this time Tex was a sawin' an' filin' his way out of jail. If she stopped playin' Jardine would get up to a barred window, that connected the jail with the front room of the house, and request a touchin' number like "My Darling Nellie Gray," an' Cora was off again. Then one night, when Tex had the hole big enough, he steps out and escapes. In the mornin', when the Sheriff comes in, there was Jardine and Lee sleepin' peaceful like, and neither of 'em knew a thing they could tell the Sheriff 'bout what had happened th' night before. When Jardine seemed to have lost interest in Cora's playin', the Sheriff dropped how Tex was able to do his sawin', and the whole town was a laughin' at Kinney and his gal.

Tex made his escape to Mono Lake on a horse he stole at a ranch in Bridgeport. He hid out for a long time, even though there was a price on his head. Then one day an Indian, who had been hidin' in ambush a long time to get Tex, got the drop on him as he was gettin' water at a spring. The Indian got the reward, and Tex got a long term in prison, where he finally died.

Joe Lee, who had shot Callahan, had his case called before Judge Briggs, who was known to be a mighty tough judge on criminals; but through the help of Lee's relatives in San Francisco, who had put up the money, he was able to get Pat Reddy to defend him. Lee got off with a sentence of nine years in San Quentin

Jail and sheriff's house in Bridgeport, California

but at the end of six months Pat Reddy had pulled enough strings to get him out, on condition that he take himself off for Mexico, which he did.

But, Lordy God, the worst miscarriage of justice of all was that Charlie Jardine got off scot free, through the influence of his gang. However, it wasn't long afore he met his match in Bodie, when he met up with Pioche Kelley. He was nicknamed "Pioche" because he had hailed from Pioche, Nevada. Pioche was known as a sure shot an' a tough ombre, and for that reason had been appointed Deputy Sheriff in Bodie, as 'twas thought he could cope with the bad element of the camp.

One night the Bodie-Hawthorne stage was robbed, an' a shipment of bullion taken off. Everything pointed to Charlie Jardine as bein' the holdup man. Pioche made his brag he would arrest him—dead or alive. The next night in the alley, back of the Sawdust Corner Saloon, both pulled their guns, but Pioche was quicker on the draw an' Charlie Jardine dropped to the sidewalk dead. Pioche was acquitted next day by the jury, an' given a vote of thanks for riddin' the camp of a character like Charlie Jardine. (I've heard, though, that Pioche Kelley never slept well after this shootin', an' used to have nightmares where he imagined Jardine was a standin' over him with a loaded gun.)

Please order another drink, Mister; seein' as how this was a long winded and excitin' story, an' I'm all out of breath. It's a true story, though, every word of it is true—as the criminal records of Mono County will show.

Lordy God! Such a lot of trouble to start over a little painted Chink girl, out in Lundy.

CHAPTER NINE

Rivalry Between the Butchers' Wives

Donnelly and Johl were both unmarried when they bought out the City Market on Main Street from the Warren Bros. Charlie Donnelly, at the time, was courting an English woman by the name of Annie Pagdin. She was an artist, and supported herself and her mother by giving painting lessons, and selling some few paintings. She was a large, haughty sort of person, who took great pride in her English ancestry. She would often say, "Hif hany of hour folks back in hold Hengland could see the way we 'ave to live 'ere in Bodie, and the people we 'ave to associate with, they would wonder what hever tempted us to come 'ere to America, and leave hour fine hold Henglish hestate." Now folks hereabouts had some doubts as to "the fine hold Henglish hestate," but they didn't have any as to the pretensions of Annie Pagdin.

When she and Donnelly were at last married he built her a nice white cottage. She proudly proceeded to fill it up with furniture, and with paintings of her own making. Some were huge paintings of scenes in Yosem-

ite Valley, but you couldn't get far enough away from
them, in those little rooms, to tell whether they were
mountains or the side of a barn; but, with each picture
she painted her fame as an artist spread around the
camp. Then she began painting dishes, with flowers
and trees and pretty girls all over them. Donnelly
had a brick oven built in the yard where she would take
the dishes after each coat of paint, and when she had
painted and baked, baked and painted, about ten times,
they were ready for use on the table. She had a servant
to do her cooking now, and, after a dinner at "The
Donnelly's," the guests came away—not talking about
the food they had eaten, or the good time they had, but
about the things that were painted on the dishes. The
Donnelly home had become the gathering place of the
"genteel set."

Then something happened that, for a time, threat-

Home of Annie Donnelly

ened to break up the partnership of Donnelly and Johl.

Eli Johl was a rough, uncouth German who spoke broken English. He had learned the butcher business in Germany, from the killing of the beast to the wrapping of it up for the customers. He knew more about the butcher business in a minute than Donnelly would know in a lifetime. Furthermore, he took the worst end of it, mostly the slaughter house work, while Charlie stood behind the counter in a white apron.

Well, Eli didn't aspire to high society, but in the evenings he would take a stroll down to the "Red Light

Interior of house of Eli and Lottie Johl

District," and drop into some place where the music was playing. When there was dancing Eli would "trip the light fantastic" with a girl named Lottie. She was an attractive, lovable girl, with soft hazel eyes, and light curly hair, and a mouth curled up in the corners that seemed to be smiling all the time. Nobody knew anything about her life, not even her name, excepting it was Lottie.

Well, Lottie grew fond of Eli—and he was plumb crazy about her. He showered her with diamonds and money, and soon they stood in front of a preacher and were married; yes, legally married, license, ring, preacher and all; and this was what nearly broke up the partnership of Donnelly and Johl.

It was more than Mrs. Donnelly could stand, having a girl of Lottie's type inflict herself on the business, but, considering all things, Charlie didn't see his way clear to dissolve the partnership. Much against his wife's opposition, and violent protests, the firm of Donnelly and Johl went on doing business; and prospering.

Eli bought his wife a cottage, of five rooms, that had been built by Osborne of the Daily Free Press, on Main Street, a few doors above the butcher shop. It was furnished in the manner of the times, velvet carpets, point lace curtains, chenille drapes, and the best sideboard and piano that was ever brought into Bodie. When it came to decorating the walls—they must have paintings. Yes, good paintings, and Lottie would do them herself. Eli reasoned, "if Annie Donnelly could make paintings, so could Lottie, teacher or no teacher, and they would have the best and most expensive frames money could buy." So Eli sent out for yards and yards of canvas, an easel and paints, and Lottie started her daubing. Eli would stand back of the easel and praise her work, with its sky of indigo blue, and ground that looked like mustard. Her first painting was a huge affair, with mountains in the background that looked, for all the world, like whopping big cones of salt—they were so white and smooth. There was a river at the base of the mountains; it was standing still, and might have been a sheet of ice—excepting on its banks were green grass and trees by the dozens. Flying across the river was a flock of dark blue ducks, and standing in the foreground was a bird that looked like something prehistoric. It had a long yellow beak, legs like a stork, and tail feathers like a peacock. Now Eli could see nothing but merit in the painting, and it was

Lottie Johl's painting

framed in a huge gold frame, with an inner band of red velvet, and hung on the wall.

Well, Lottie persisted, spurred on by the praises of her husband, until she had filled all the walls with pictures. No one ever came to their home, so Eli was the only one who ever looked at them. Lottie's past had followed her into the little red house, and she was shunned by all those who called themselves respectable. She spent lonely hours, and at times her mind must have gone back to the days that were filled with romance, gaiety, and excitement; but now she was a wife, and she would remain true to Eli. She would show Annie Donnelly that a woman can reform; but Annie's feelings toward her grew worse instead of better.

A grand masquerade ball was advertised in the paper, to be given in the Miners' Union Hall. Eli hit upon a plan. He would send to Goldstein's in San Francisco and get the very finest costume they had, for Lottie. She would go to the masquerade shining and resplendent, so that the people would really gasp. Then, when she unmasked, they would be carried away with her beauty. Yes, siree, the masquerade ball would be Lottie's "coming out in society."

When she came into the hall in this costume people *did* gasp. The like of it had never been seen in Bodie before—or after. The dress was a white satin, all covered with seed pearls and diamonds (just imitations, of course), but a sparkling like the real thing. On her blonde curls was set a crown made of the same kind of diamonds and pearls. Soon heads got together, and the speculating started as to who she could be. You see, no one suspected it was Lottie, because it wasn't supposed she would ever try to break into polite society this way.

Besides, not many people of the so-called "respectable element" had ever seen her.

Then a committee was appointed to award prizes for the most beautiful costume. Of course, they agreed to give it to the "lady" in the bejeweled dress. When the bugle blew for the unmasking at midnight, she was seen to hesitate a minute; then she slipped off her mask, and her eyes had a little frightened look. The fellow she was dancing with recognized her, and he just strolled off and left her a standing in the middle of the hall. She moved quietly to the side, by herself, and sat down. When the committee, who was to award the prizes, found that it had selected Lottie Johl for the first prize, they were in a great state of consternation. Of course, they couldn't award the prize to a girl like Lottie. It wouldn't look right in the paper when they published the list of prize winners. It would hurt the prestige of their organization, too. Now that they knew who she was, Lottie shouldn't be allowed to stay any longer at the dance. They appointed two of their committee to ask Lottie to leave. The committee then announced that they needed more time to decide the awarding of the prizes, and had the orchestra strike up a waltz: It was the only time no one asked Lottie to dance, and she sat—sort of looking into space. Then the two men from the committee came up and said a few hurried words (that no one else heard but Lottie) and she rose quietly and walked toward the front door. Those who were standing there said she had tears in her eyes, but as she went out she looked neither to the right nor to the left.

Eli hadn't gone to the dance, as he knew it would be a dead give-away that Lottie was there; besides he knew he wouldn't be able to keep his eyes from following her.

But, when she reported to him what had happened, she had to restrain him from going up and cleaning out the hall. He swore, and he stamped, and he raved, and he threatened he would get even on the people of Bodie.

Next morning, when they talked things over, they decided it was best for Eli to keep mum about the whole affair, as he could not help matters. Then, too, it might give Annie Donnelly a lot of happiness if she knew just how they felt.

So Eli and Lottie lived on for a number of years in their little cottage, just keeping to themselves. Their loneliness seemed to draw them closer together as time went on.

One day Lottie felt ill. The doctor was called and

Lottie's grave

gave a prescription to be filled at the local drug store. That night Lottie was taken with violent convulsions. The doctor was called again. He was unable to understand the sudden change in his patient. In the morning Lottie was dead.

The town was a buzzing with excitement; "Lottie Johl had committed suicide." Everyone, excepting Eli, believed it. He demanded that an autopsy be performed, and what it disclosed was the most astonishing thing of all. The prescription in the drug store had been put up wrong. A deadly drug had been given to Lottie, instead of the medicine ordered. It was not intentional, on the part of the druggist, but just plain carelessness. Nothing was done about it, as the town was too busy quarreling about where Lottie should be buried. Some said she should be put in the "outcast cemetery." Others contended, on account of her keeping straight all the years she was married to Eli, she should at least be given a place "inside the fence." Finally a compromise was made, to the effect that

"Lottie" (Johl)

Lottie could be buried in the very last place in the upper cemetery; and so it was. Eli put a high wrought iron fence around her grave—the best of any to be found on cemetery hill.

When the following Memorial Day drew near Eli kept thinking of what he could do to draw attention to Lottie's grave, and make the people of Bodie sorry they had treated his darling in such a heartless way. They should be brought to know that Lottie was really an angel, and had been treated like an outcast. So he got a local carpenter to build a canopy that would go over her grave, fence and all; and with his own hands Eli decorated it. He wrapped it first with buntin' of red, white and blue, with little flags here and there, and then entwined it with paper flowers of all descriptions. At the head of the grave he placed an enlarged picture of

Lottie's painting in Museum at Bodie

his darling. It was done in colors, showing her blonde hair, blue eyes, diamond earrings, and dress of lace. Yes! when the people of Bodie gazed on that picture they would have to feel sorry they had treated Lottie in such a cruel way.

On Memorial Day, Eli had everything in readiness. He stationed himself near the iron railing and waited for folks to come his way. They did come, in *droves,* drawn mostly by curiosity, to see what they called "Eli's Carnival Booth," but before they went away many eyes had tears in them. They were *not* especially sorry for their treatment of Lottie, but Eli's grief and love really touched their hearts.

Eli stayed on for many years, living alone in a little five-room cottage, with the pictures on the wall and everything as it used to be, excepting Lottie wasn't there. He even looked forward to Memorial Day, the putting up of the canopy, and the placing of her pho-

Annie Donnelly's masterpiece

tograph at the head of the grave. Some way it seemed like *his* day; the day he took on importance, and when no one passed him and Lottie without stopping.

At last the day came when Donnelly told Eli he had enough money; he was going to retire. He and Annie were moving to Burlingame, where they would build themselves a grand home, with even a picture gallery in it, where Annie's paintings could be hung.

Eli bought out Donnelly's interest, and ran the butcher business alone for some years. On the decline of the camp, he suddenly decided he, too, would leave Bodie. He sold the little cottage just as it was, paintings and all, and he even left the enlarged picture of Lottie hanging there with the rest.

Eli was never heard from again. Rumors came back that he had been killed in a train wreck.

Lottie's picture afterwards hung back of a local bar. It was pretty enough to hang any place. Then a boarding house keeper, named Josie Pearl, coaxed it away from the saloon man, and hung it on the wall of her dining room. That way it was saved from the fire of 1932. Now it has found a place in the old museum in Bodie, above one of Lottie's own paintings; and Lottie's eyes seem to be gazing on a large painting hanging on the wall across the room. It is Annie Donnelly's masterpiece—of Yosemite Falls.

CHAPTER TEN

Jim Pender's Story of Buffalo Bill

The hardest boiled old son of a gun this town ever knowed was one they nicknamed "Buffalo Bill," account of his white beard and his tales of how he'd fought Indians. His real name was William Gross, and he used to tell that on the Isle of Man, where he hailed from, they used to address him as Mister. Well, Mister or no Mister on the Isle of Man, he was just plain Buffalo Bill here in Bodie, and sometimes just Buff, and sometimes old thievin', liar Bill. He was the slickest petty thief the town had ever knowed. Why, he was so good in plyin' an' teachin' his trade that he trained his old hound dog to help him. If he went into a store and a plug of tobaccy, or any sizeable thing, happened to be on the counter, down to the floor it would go, an' when he got back to his cabin there the old hound would be lyin' in front of the door with it still in his teeth. He always kept some naked bones on the top shelf to reward th' dog for bein' a good accomplice.

One day old Buff spied a package, all done up neat like, on the counter of Bryant and West's store. It didn't matter what it contained, he figured he could use it. So he edged around 'till the clerk wasn't lookin' —an' down it went. The hound grabbed it an' made his getaway, but he hadn't gone far afore the string broke an' the paper came off; so the dog just picked up the white thing that fell out an' kept on a goin'. When Buffalo Bill got home there was th' dog a holdin' a woman's white drawers in his teeth, an' they was all trimmed with lace and a floatin' in the breeze like a flag o' truce. Now Bill was a sure enough woman hater, so a kick in the head was all the poor old hound got that day for his trouble.

The cabin was piled from floor to ceiling with everything Buff *didn't* need. You could dig out anything from an anvil and bellows to a mine car and broken rocking chair. He brought home everything and anything that he found lyin' around loose in the camp. At last things got so crowded that he decided he needed to build an addition; so he dug a cave in the hill behind the shack and connected the two together by a tunnel made of timbers and covered with dirt. He moved most of the stuff into the cave, an' was ready to go on his way again a sneakin' and a stealin'.

His name got to be such a bug-a-boo in the camp that parents used to threaten their children, that if they didn't do this an' that, old Buffalo Bill would come an' steal 'em; an' th' children would run like all get out if they saw him blocks away.

Often he went on prospectin' trips into the surroundin' mountains, lockin' his door with three different locks, an' leavin' his old dog on the inside with a pile of potatoes an' bones beside 'im, to keep 'im from starvin'. When he came back he never failed to show a

Buffalo Bill of Bodie

rich rock, an' some unsuspectin' person would put up a grub stake. He undertook one time to interest a hard rock miner in his new prospect. The miner turned the rock over an' over, and, lookin' old Bill squarely in the eye, he said, "You old lyin', cheatin' son of a bitch, this ain't no hillside rock, it's highgrade from the Fortuna ledge, and I've a good notion to crack your old lyin' skull wide open with it. You get to hell out o' here," an' old Bill wasn't long in gettin'. But he still stuck to old Jim Townsend's contention, that all you need to make a good mine is a hole in the ground and a good liar. So he plied his trade for years, and always found a sucker who would bite. He told 'em all, "If I don't make you a millionaire out of this prospect, I hope I'll go to hell when I die." Now I contend there must have been more 'an one hell to accommodate old Bill.

Wood was generally scarce in the winter, and, some of those 40° below zero times, a good wood pile was worth more than a good pile of money in the bank. There wasn't no place to store the wood generally, but out in the open; so if anyone tampered with the wood pile over night there was always telltale tracks in th' snow. More than once there were peculiar footmarks found around a wood stack in the mornin' an' big hollow places where big sticks had been yanked out. People had their suspicions; but havin' a suspicion an' catchin' a thief is two different things. So finally a trap was set for old Bill. A hole was drilled in a log of wood an' a stick of giant powder was put in the place. It wasn't long afore that certain stick of wood was gone.

One cold day in winter old Bill an' his dog was a snoozin' by the fire when BANG! the whole front of the shack was blowed out, and Bill found hisself outside in th' snow, with all his ill-gotten goods a flyin' 'round him. Lordy God! Bill was so black from soot an' powder even th' old singed hound hardly knew 'im.

He went about rebuildin' the old shack soon as he could, sleepin' in th' cave until he had it finished. Made it even bigger than it was afore—case he might see somethin' lyin' around that he needed.

CHAPTER ELEVEN

"Ould" Lady O'Brien and Her Son "Moike"

"Moike, will you come help me shake up the feathers. Some way I can't handle this tick anny more. It's been a long, long time since I raised the chickens in the ould country whose feathers went into this bed, a—long—long time."

Mike helped, as requested, and then his mother sat down on a trunk nearby and went into one of her reminiscent moods.

She was fat, round-faced, with sharp blue eyes, and a droll-looking mouth. She had a habit of shutting her eyes and wrinkling up her face when anything especially pleased her. No one could be mistaken as to her nationality. The Irish look, the brogue, the wit, were all hers.

Mike was small in stature, sharp featured, and had a dark moustache.

"Moike, I've seen a lot of trouble since I landed in this country from County Kerry—a—lot of trouble and some happiness, too. Here you and I and Stephie are the only ones left out of a family of ten. We never see or hear from Stephie, Moike. He never was much of a hand to write. There's some of the others buried in Ireland, some in Mariposy on the Mother Lode, and your father, God be with him, is here in Bodie on the hillside. Shure I can see his grave every day from the kitchen winder.''

Here her voice approached something of a wail. It was genuine grief.

''Once, Moike, when you were a baby, the doctor tot you were going to die. Now you're fifty years of age and never done a good day's work in awl your life.'' (Quick was the change from grief to anger.) ''Shure I tot I would lose the whole woruld if I lost you.'' Then, shaking her fist menacingly, she added: ''and God only knows how well off I'd bin if I had.''

Mike took his mother's railings in a philosophical way. They came ever so often and he was used to them. He was willing to put up with her Irish temper, remembering that she had a good nest egg in the bank.

They lived in a little cottage, of five rooms, on Fuller Street. It was not uncomfortable but contained only the bare necessities. The kitchen stove was the thing most prized by Ellen of all her possessions. The trademark ''Mariposa'' stood out in bold relief on the oven door. She used to point at it with pride and say, ''Shure me and the stove both came from 'Mariposy'. That was the place I landed in when I came from Ireland, and Steve, my husband, was looking for gold.''

Mike generally came under his mother's displeasure every month when the bill came in from the corner grocery store. For, although Ellen could not read or write, in some way she kept accurate account of what the bill should be. She asked the price of every article not once, but twice; and knew to a penny what she owed. If Mike padded the bill by buying a bottle or two or three of whiskey, of which he was fond, the old lady was sure to find it out, and he was in for a tongue lashing. This he took good naturedly, and considered it none too high a price to pay for value received.

"Ould" Ellen had a hobby. It *was chickens.* They all had names, and, being a mixed breed, each laid a different looking egg. She would proudly display them in a dish on the parlor table, and explain to all visitors, "Shure this is Blackie's egg, and this one is the White Angel's. I've had her ever since I came to Bodie, and she lays the finest, biggest and whitest egg of anny hen in the camp. This is Dora's, they're always speckled," and so on.

As time went on she began to hide the eggs in all the nooks and crannies in the house, taking as much care to select her hiding places as if she were caching a horde of gold. The locked trunk, whose key reposed in the deep recess of her bosom, the bureau drawers, the stocking bag, the old chip barrel, were among her hiding places.

"If I don't hide them," she explained, "Moike will be afther selling them for whisky. You can't be up to the thricks of that spalpeen Moike." Occasionally she forgot the hiding places, and also the date of vintage, so consequently the eggs were often brought forth and opened with the most odoriferous and appalling result. "Moike" was even accused at times of stealing the eggs and taking them to the "Fancies" (ladies of ill repute), in order to establish himself in their favor. In fact, when anything in the house was mislaid and could not be found, "Moike" was always under suspicion.

He and his mother were not on speaking terms for some time when her best muslin nightgown could not be found. Her suspicions were conveyed to all the neighbors: "Sure some Fancy, down in Virgin Alley, is putting on style with it now. It had so many foine, foine tucks in the yoke, and nice handmade lace awl up around the high neck and the cuffs of the sleeves, arrah! arrah! I wouldn't have been wearin' it myself, but it was afther turnin' yellow it had lain so long in the trunk. Bad cess to the day I ever unlocked the trunk and took it out." When the nightgown finally was found she scrutinized it closely and came to the conclusion that it *had been* worn by somebody besides herself. "But," she added, "he got afraid and had to get it back."

One day she was visiting a friend whom she had not seen for some time. On the table was a pot of soup boiling on the electric plate. She bent down and looked under the plate with a puzzled expression on her face, and asked, "and phare tell me is the fire?" "There is no fire, it's boiling by electricity." "And phat, by awl the saints, is electricity?" she asked. The good neighbor became so entangled and confused, in trying to explain the development of electricity, that she simplified matters by getting down to the source. "Well, anyway, Mrs. O'Brien, it's the snow melting in the Green Creek Canyon that's boiling the soup." Old Ellen looked skeptical, then mystified, and exclaimed, "Mighty, mighty, you Americans do strange things."

She was timid with strangers, and preferred to associate only with the Irish of the camp, or with their descendants, who had "preserved the faith."

At times it was necessary for her to go to the bank

and draw some money, and put her mark ("X") on the withdrawal slip. On these occasions she wore a black crinoline dress, that stuck out like a balloon. On her head was the "mourning bonnet," a small hat with yards and yards of black crepe, which hung down her back to her waist; and sometimes, when caught by the wind, floated behind like an ominous black cloud. She had bought the bonnet when Stephen, her husband, had died, and always called it her "widdy's weeds."

On one occasion she found herself quite disturbed and baffled on the intricacies of what might be called a verbal inheritance. One Hughie Gorman, who was going to San Francisco for medical attention, had given "Moike" the key to his cabin, with the remark, "Here, Mike, is the key to the house. If I don't happen to come back the shack is yours." Well, Hughie didn't come back. He died in San Francisco a few weeks later. Mike, who made no attempt to claim the shack and put it up for rent, was called "a know-nothin' " and a "Ne'er-do-well" by the old lady. Finally she decided to take matters into her own hands, and "have the deed recorded, just to make things clear and straight." When told by the Recorder that a deed was a written paper, the old lady went into a tantrum. "Glory! glory, what is this world coming to anyway! Sure you wouldn't even take a man's word when he's dead. Didn't he put the key in Moike's hand and say, 'Moike, if I don't come back the cabin is yours'? Now write that on your books as I'm tellin' it, and I'll give you the two dollars for recordin' the deed, which I am sure is awl you were afther in the first place."

Then one day word was received that her son Stevie had met with a tragic death in southern Nevada. Old

Ellen was heart broken. For months the neighborhood was disturbed by her keening (a sort of low cry at first, which gradually gained crescendo until it became a high pitched wail). She could not be comforted. When her grief had somewhat subsided, she and Mike would sit for days without even speaking.

She finally took to looking at the albums of family pictures, and as she gazed on each face she would review the birth, the life, the death of each one separately, even if there was no one to hear what she was saying. Yes—"auld" Ellen had a—lot—of trouble.

Her strength was gradually failing. She did not eat regularly, the eggs were not gathered, the amount of the grocery bill did not interest her any more. Mike was able to get more and more liquor, and he often went to bed in a drunken stupor.

At times she sent him up to the cemetery to see "if the graves were all right." He would come back with the report, "Sure, they're there in the same place, mother, but a damn tight squeeze you're going to have to get in beside father. Old lady McQuade spread out so far when they planted her you won't have much room."

Ellen finally suffered a stroke, and was bedridden for some time. The parish priest came often and gave her spiritual consolation and comfort. She gave all directions as to how she should be buried. The black crinoline dress was to enshroud her and her "Widdy's Weeds" and shoes to be placed in her casket at the foot, "just in case I need them, dear."

Mike survived his mother by less than a year.

The house gradually went to ruin and decay. The roof fell in. The windows were broken from their sashes. Strangers roamed through the empty rooms; came in one open doorway and went out through another.

One summer afternoon a terrific whirlwird came tearing down from the hillside. It struck the "ould lady's" house with great fury. The walls of the building suddenly collapsed, and from the mattress, which had been torn open by treasure seekers, arose a cloud of feathers—that circled high in the air and then settled lightly on the landscape.

They were Ellen's "ould country feathers," that had served their purpose.

CHAPTER TWELVE

The Bodie Fire Department and Stealing of the Fire Bell

On August 10, 1941, the community was terribly disturbed on discovering the old bronze fire bell had been stolen from the belfry of the firehouse.

Many a time had its clear, clanging alarm brought the volunteer fire department out; sometimes in the dead of night, sometimes in the cold gray dawn of morning, or the heat of a drowsy afternoon.

This old bell was a RELIC. It had sounded the alarm for many minor conflagrations, and for the two disastrous fires of Bodie which were forty years apart, the one in 1892 and the last in 1932. Each time the firehouse had been burned, but the bell had been found in the debris as unimpaired, and as clear-toned as the day it was cast. New firehouses had been built, and again the crowning feature was the bronze bell—poised in the belfry. People of the town, all living in wooden structures built fifty or sixty years ago, felt a sense of security knowing it was there.

However, now one can look through the empty belfry, which has been torn apart, and it is like a cage whose bird has flown. Something loved by the residents, and vitally important to their security, has been taken away.

There is one small thread of a clue as to who the vandals might be, and, if through it, the bell is recovered I will write the circumstances under a later date.

The Bodie Volunteer Fire Department was one of the first organizations of the boom days of '78. It was a bucket brigade. A hundred or more narrow black rubber buckets hung on the frame of the hook and ladder cart. The engine and hose carts were separate.

There was Babcock Engine Co. No. 1; Hook & Ladder Co. No. 1; Champion Hose Co. No. 1; Neptune Hose Co. No. 2; Neptune Hook & Ladder Co. No. 2.

The firemen drilled regularly, and were well organized. The officers wore red rubberized hats and belts, with emblems emblazoned on them showing the official office of the wearer.

('Twas whispered that it wasn't hard to get men to volunteer to join the fire department, as they were therefore exempt from jury duty at the County Seat at Bridgeport.)

During later years a Scotchman named Hughie Gorham held the office of Chief; and took his duties very seriously. He called a meeting immediately after every fire, and the firemen, sometimes dripping wet, had to attend. The order of the procedure went something like this:

"Who was the first *mon* here?"

"I was, Chief."

"Well, you should be, you're the youngest an' the strongest."

"Who was the second mon?"

"I was, Chief."

"Well, you should be; you live the closest to the fire-house."

"Who was the third mon?"

A half dozen voices this time.

"No, I'll be damned if you were, *I* was the third mon myself, and all of you were trailin' behind me, and most of you are about half my age."

Those who were not present to answer roll call, unless they had a valid reason, were fined.

The annual Firemen's Grand Ball was an elaborate and gala event.

When marching in the 4th of July, and other parades, the members of the Volunteer Fire Department made a most imposing spectacle, dressed in their regalia, and pulling their fire engine and hook and ladder and hose carts.

Fire house with bell missing from belfry

Until now this old fire bell had remained as the most outstanding symbol of the colorful past *glory* of Bodie's fire department.

*   *   *   *   *

September 28, 1941.
The Fire Bell Has Been Recovered.
The slender clue was a good and only one.

On the afternoon of August 10th, four boys, presumably between the ages of 19 and 21, came into town in a red open car. The writer of this story, by way of making their trip interesting, was showing them some gold specimens and relics, and picked up a miner's candlestick, beautifully hand wrought. Mentioning the name of the man who made it, I remarked that he should have been a manufacturing jeweler instead of a blacksmith. One of the boys, overcome with pride, said, "He was my grandfather." Knowing the family, I inquired to which daughter he belonged, and he told me. The car was still there after dark, parked across the street from the firehouse. The next morning foot tracks led across the street from the firehouse to where this car had been parked.

I wrote to this boy's mother, explaining the matter in the most diplomatic way I could.

I received a joint letter from both parents, telling me they had located the fire bell and would send it back at their expense.

No questions were asked, and no charges were preferred against the boys, as they were all of draft age and the citizens of Bodie wanted them to enter the service with a clean record.

It was afterwards rumored that a millionaire, who

owned a big estate in Southern California, had hired the boys to come and get the bell for him.

So the bell was restored to its old home in the belfry. May it rest there in peace, as just an ornament to the firehouse, without ringing out the alarm for any more disastrous fires.

Again in 1954 an attempt was made to steal the fire bell. It was being put into the back of a truck bearing a Nevada license when the thieves were detected.

Father Cassin

CHAPTER THIRTEEN

Story of Father Cassin

Come on strangers an' buy me a drink of whisky; yes, two, three, four drinks, if you think my stories are worth it, afore you start your sight seein' around the old ghost town. I'm used to drinkin' whisky an' I ain't worth nothin' now-a-days without it. I'm so broke up to see the old camp the way it is today I have to have whisky, an' a lot of it, to blot out the present an' bring back the past. Thank you, Mister, that's three now an' enough to get me goin'.

The stories I have to tell you all happened in the rip roarin', hell bent minin' camps of Bodie and Lundy, 'round in the '80's an' later.

Now you wouldn't think it of me, but my startin' off story has to do with religion. Don't snicker, please, Miss, at heart I'm really a Christian, an' I still contend that religion can exist under a time beaten, whisky hardened old hide.

It was about '78 that a young priest came to these parts. His name was John B. Cassin, and he was just out of the seminary. Think of the Bishop sendin' a young, inexperienced missionary up to a hell roarin' camp like Bodie. Well, he proved equal to the task, an' afore he left he'd received a liberal education on human nature in the rough. Comin' in on the stage coach he was sittin' opposite a sportin' woman an' a gambler. It was a cold day in winter an' the father had a big muffler wrapped around his church collar, but when the talk went to the point where it offended him, he pulled off his muffler an' asserted himself. Not another word was spoken until the stage pulled into Bodie.

When the news was spread around that a real sky pilot had invaded the camp, some rejoiced, some sneered. He had been commissioned to build a Catholic church, so he set out to do it, and later on he found the people were more generous than pious. The funds were quickly subscribed, an' a site for the church was given by the minin' company. It was on a rocky hillside on the eastern slope of town; but from there on Father Cassin's difficulties increased. He seemed to be left to his own resources as to plannin', architecture, etc. He could be seen pacin' up and down over the rocky hillside, where the church was to be built, in a befuddled sort of way, and if some kind hearted carpenters hadn't taken pity on him he would probably be walkin' around there yet.

Well, after a time the church stood completed, a very plain sort of buildin' with a steep, slantin' roof an' lots of windows, an' a heap larger than was needed for th' people who attended.

It was generally so cold in winter durin' services that the congregation did ample penance for their sins.

The bishop had told the father to honor the man who had done the most towards its construction, so he called it St. John's, after hisself.

Father Cassin was called on many a time to go to the dyin', those who died in bed, an' those who died with their boots on. At one time he was called after a shootin' fracas. The feller with a bullet in him was lyin' on the saloon floor in a pool of blood. When the priest bent over him he thought it was his adversary comin' at him, again he pulled the trigger of his gun, an' the bullet went just over the priest's head.

Many a time a dispute that would have ordinarily ended in gun play was left to him to settle; yes—siree, Father Cassin was known to be fair an' unprejudiced.

Great amusement was caused in the camp at one time over a mixup in a double chistenin'. Two "Dago" women, who were great friends, decided to have their babies christened at the same time. One child was a boy, the other a girl. The mother of the boy was to be Godmother to the baby girl, and vice versa. Well, when they stood in front of the priest, each was holdin' th' baby of the other woman. Father Cassin asked: "And what name, please, for your baby?" "Antone,"

Cross in Bodie Museum

said the woman who was holdin' the girl, thinkin' he meant th' name for that there kid of hers. "Florence," said the other woman, when asked the same question. So Antone was baptized Florence and Florence was baptized Antone. Let St. Peter untangle that muddle.

Lordy God! It's actually told for a fact that at another christenin' the holy water froze so hard it left an icicle hangin' on the baby's chin.

Father Cassin brought his sister as a housekeeper for him. She was a spinster lady, an' a fine dressmaker. She made the finest pleatin's an' polonaise of any seamstress in the camp. Her bustles were works of art, all padded and pleated like, that gave their wearer the effect of havin' a waist like a wasp, an' hips like an elephant.

Father Cassin stayed here for five years, an' always counted 'em as the most excitin' and interestin' years of his career. Afterwards, when he was pastor in Santa Rosa, he was often called on at public gatherin's to tell his experiences of the wild and lawless days in Bodie.

When he died he had been in Holy Orders longer than any other priest in California.

The Catholic church burned down some time around '28. 'Twas whispered it was set afire by a feller who wanted to buy it for the lumber in it and couldn't make a deal; but the big wooden cross on top fell away from the buildin', as if in protest, an' was found several days afterwards in the sagebrush. Seems as if it wanted to remain as a souvenir, testifyin' for religion in this outpost of civilization.

The cross was found by Robert Conway, an old and respected resident of Bodie, and is now on display in the Bodie Museum.

CHAPTER FOURTEEN

The Editor's Story

Some years ago when we were living in Oakland we decided that Martin, the faithful watchman in Bodie, should have a vacation. My husband and I came up to stay while he was gone.

On a beautiful moonlight night in June we took him to Bridgeport to catch the stage going into Reno. As we rode back into Bodie, Victor remarked that we should ride up on the Standard hill to see if everything was all right around the mill. It was during the last shutdown in the old camp and we were about the only people in town. We stopped on top of the hill and my husband got out and went to the mill. I sat admiring the beauty of the night and enjoying the gentle breeze, and I was impressed by the fact that I could even discern the White Mountains, a distance of about ninety miles. Finally Victor came back and got into the car, which stubbornly refused to go. Now all my husband knows about a car is to get out and say, "Come on now, old Betsy," and start shaking it, hoping if there is a loose wire it will connect. He shook and shook old Betsy, but she didn't move. He finally raised the hood and started to tinker around the engine. He then suggested to me that it would be better for me to start walking down the hill, as my pace was slower than his, and he would either overtake me in the car or by walking.

As I went over a cattle guard a little way down, the irons rattled in a sort of loud, uncanny way. I had gone over them hundreds of times but they had never sounded like *that* before. I quickened my pace a little, and, looking over on Cemetery Hill, the headstones glistening in the moonlight, they looked bigger and whiter, and there were more of them. They had never looked like *that* before. I was nearing a deserted building now, with doors and windows out. When I reached it the moonlight was streaming through it in a weird sort of way. I quickened my steps a little. The next vacant building I passed, there was a white cloth ceiling hanging down in the front room. It was moving back and forth from the breeze coming in through the broken windows. I could feel my heart beating wildly. As I neared the third building a loose piece of tin on the roof was rattling and there seemed to be a dark form in the shadow of the building. I started running, and finally realized someone behind me was running, too. At last I stumbled—and my husband caught me in his arms. "What's the matter with you, anyway?" he asked. I couldn't answer, and he took me by the arm. As we entered the house I looked back, and realized that after all these years I had suddenly caught the spirit of the Old Ghost Town.

CHAPTER FIFTEEN

Jim Pender's Story of Mary McCann

Lordy God, plenty of Irish drifted into this old camp in its day. There were the O'Briens, the Brodigans, the Fayheys, the Hallihans, the Sullivans, and hundreds of others. Guess that's what made it such an' up an' goin' concern. Fact is, the old payrolls looked like a roster from Ireland.

'Mong those who heard the call of Bodie an' answered it was Mary McCann. She was a rawboned Irish woman, who had been brought out to this country as a servant for the Tobin family of the Hibernia Bank of San Francisco.

On comin' to Bodie, Mary hired out as janitor of the school and different lodge halls of the town.

(Pour me a drink, Mister. I need it.)

She built herself a little shack on the lot adjoinin' the brewery owned by Nick Carion, and from that day on the feudin' started between 'em.

'Twasn't long afore the Bodieites began to realize that Mary had a tongue sharper 'an a razor, an' she meant it when she said she "didn't fear man, beast, or the devil."

"Bad cess to the day," she would say, "that I ever bo't a house alongside of that German pig of a Carion an' his trollop of a wife. They're always throwin' the slops in the direction of me house, an' that ain't awl; ould Carion goes up on the hill, back of me house, an' turns the wather so that it runs into me cellar and fills it up. Shurin I'll get meself a shovel an' I'll fix him."

Fact of the matter is, Mary's house was built in a sort of draw, where the water just naturally drains down the hill in the spring, an' the seepage comes up in the cellar, as it does in many other places in town.

Well, Lordy God, Mary buys herself a shovel, an' soon she has a moat dug all around her shack. Then she goes up the side hill and begins divertin' the water so as it runs down into the Carion lot an' cellar. Old Nick comes out with blood in his eye an' the fightin' starts. Mary calls him all the names in the calendar, an' when he answers back, Mary reaches down in her pocket an' whips out a gun, firin' two shots that go wide of the mark, but which puts old Nick dead on th' run. He goes down to the Justice Court an' swears out a warrant for Mary's arrest.

Now the Deputy Sheriff at this time is a sort of a timid fellow named Henry Hartley, an' Lordy God, when Henry hears he has to arrest Mary McCann he gets weak all over; but it's up to him to do it or give up his badge. Sort o' tremblin' like, he goes up th' street with a crowd followin' at his heels to see th' fun. Th' moat Mary has dug around her shanty is filled with water, but Henry wades through it an' raps faint like on Mary's door, callin' for her to come out. Mary opens th' door, an' answers him by cussin' all th' so and so's of law enforcin' officers in the county, an' she tells him

to go over next door where he ought to go an' arrest
that old son of a B of a Carion.

Hartley keeps a pleadin' sort of easy like for her to
come out an' not make a fuss. Then Mary, seein' th'
crowd that has followed Hartley, an' how they are sort
o' snickerin' at him, decides she will make him more of
a laughin' stock than ever by suggestin' that if he
wants to arrest her he will have to carry her on his
back over the "wather," as she has nothin' on her feet
but slippers. Well Hartley sort o' hesitated, not likin'
the idea, but he finally stoops down an' old Mary gets
on his back, tellin' him he's nothin' but an ass anyway,
an' over the moat they come. When he lets her down
on the other side th' crowd is a bustin' its sides with
laughter.

The next day Mary, who has bailed herself out over

Mary McCann's house today

night, appears before the Justice of the Peace. When 4 o'clock comes Mary gets up an' starts for the door. "Sit down," says the Judge. "Ah to hell wid you," says Mary, "it's time for school to be out an' I have me work to do, instead of sittin' here listenin' to your blatherin'." "Twenty dollar fine," says the Judge, an' out walks Mary, givin' th' door such a bang she almost takes it off its hinges.

When the water starts runnin' next spring it's th' same story, only the arrestin' of Mary this time is done by a little Irishman named Jack O'Brien, Hartley resignin' afore he would go up to Mary's shanty to arrest her a second time.

Jack puts handcuffs on Mary, an' leads her through th' main street, while she is a tellin' him all th' way what his mother was, an' how Ireland should have dropped into the ocean th' day a damned scallawag like him was born.

This time she is tried before Justice Holmes. "Your name, please," says the Judge. "Damn well you know me name," says Mary. "Now, Miss McCann, answer the questions asked by the court, or you'll be in contempt," says the Judge. "There you go now," says Mary, "in one breath you asks me, me name, an' in th' next you'r callin' me Miss McCann." "Order in the Court," raps the Judge. "Where do you live, Miss McCann?" "In Bodie," says Mary, "an' a damned poor place it is, I'm afther tellin' ye." "Miss McCann, do you plead guilty or not guilty of firing a shot at Nick Carion?" "Sure an' I fired a shot at the dirty bastard, an' awl I wish was that I could have killed him." "Fifty dollar fine," says the Judge.

Old Carion's health is a breakin' under the strain

of never knowin' when a shot would whizz, through
his head or past it, so he sells the brewery to a man
named John McKenzie, but neglects to tell McKenzie
that a first class feud goes with the sale.

Now Mary is antagonized even by the sight of the
brewery, and its occupants make her blood boil and her
tongue loose. McKenzie isn't there a week afore he
knows he has paid too much for that brewery.

(Another drink, please, Mister; Mary's story sort
o' demands it.)

Well, McKenzie has Mary arrested again and again
for usin' obscene language, an' assault with a deadly
weapon. Mary pays her fine, which keeps gettin' more
and more each time she is arrested, an' then she goes
at it again. She says, "What better way can I spend
my money than by shootin' at McKenzie?" She is
bound over for trial, to the Superior Court in Bridgeport this time, an' a larger fine is imposed, an' she puts
up bail to keep the peace.

Then, Lordy God, one day she gets the shock of her
life. She sees the windows of the brewery bein' boarded
up. Could the McKenzies be leavin? Mary can't believe
it. She found out, by askin' down town, that they were
really goin' to Oakland to live. The brewery business is
done for. Mary, peerin' through the lace curtains in
her shack, sees their belongin's all bein' loaded on a
freight team. Yes, there is no mistakin', they are really
leavin'. She sits there a long time, thinkin' an' lookin'
into space. The next day she sees 'em gettin' into the
stage coach, and when the driver says "Giddup," and
cracks his whip, Mary goes out an' fires a partin' shot
at 'em, but she well knows there is nothin' left in Bodie
to make life worth while for her.

She goes up on th' hill an' walks around. The water is runnin', an' there is her shovel that she used yesterday, but she doesn't pick it up. Instead she starts gatherin' some odds an' ends of boards, and soon she is nailin' them over her windows.

She leaves the next mornin' on the stage, an' overtakes the McKenzies at Hawthorne, Nevada, where they are waitin' to ship their freight. She stands back of McKenzie when he buys his tickets for Oakland; then she buys hers for San Francisco.

But, Lordy God, durin' that trip to the coast everybody on that train has McKenzie pointed out to 'em, and hears what a so and so he is, and how he has tormented and persecuted a poor lone woman who was tryin' to make a decent livin' up in Bodie.

CHAPTER SIXTEEN

Story of Pretty Maggie and Tong Sing Wo

When the Chinese invaded Bodie, along in '79, they didn't come straggling in twos and threes at a time, they descended like a big yellow horde—and they left about the same way. They all belonged to one Company, and that may have accounted for there being no tong wars in Bodie's China Town.

This story is about an Indian girl, a pretty little thing named Maggie. Too bad she had the misfortune to meet up with the big boss of China Town, Tong Sing Wo. It happened in an innocent sort of way, just because she had a craving for a bright silk handkerchief for her head.

Her mother died when she was a baby, and her grandparents, old Jim and Annie, took her to raise. Many times, when food was scarce, old Jim and Annie went hungry so that Maggie could have enough—but she never knew it.

Indians seldom keep any track of time, but Pretty Maggie must have been about sixteen years old when this story opens. Anyway, she was old enough to help

Annie pan the rock on the dumps. One day they had a streak of good luck, Annie had found a piece of high-grade, and Soderling, the assayer, had given her $15.00 for their "panning" that day. Now Maggie could buy the silk handkerchief she'd been waiting for so long.

When Maggie walked into the big merchandise establishment of Tong Sing Wo, in China Town, next day, she was sort of bewildered, never having been in a place like that before. She hesitated a minute, and then turned like she was going out again. A China boy, who was working there, stepped up and asked her what she wanted. "Yes, they had some 'velly' nice silk handkerchiefs, Missy"; and he led her to a counter across the room. How her eyes stuck out when she saw those handkerchiefs, all embroidered in birds and flowers and all colors of the rainbow. She never knew there *were* such handkerchiefs. She picked up first one and then another, trying to make a selection.

Tong Sing Wo was across the store, doing some figuring by throwing wooden rings back and forth on a wire frame, then his eyes fell on Pretty Maggie. His hands stopped operating and he stared at her for a full minute. Then his eyes took on a strange look, and he glided around the counter to where the China boy was standing. He'd take the sale, he told him, in Chinese, and the boy walked away.

Pretty Maggie liked a yellow handkerchief, and tied it under her chin. Then Tong Sing Wo told her he wasn't going to take any money for it. He said he owned the store, and he was always glad to give something to anyone who came in for the first time. Maggie was amazed—that this could be the big boss of China Town that was talking to her in such a pleasant way.

In fact, she was sort of knocked speechless, and, not even thanking him, she "guessed she'd go." He hoped she'd come back the next day, he told her, just to tell him if she really liked the handkerchief.

She *did* come back the next day, and the next day, and nearly every day after that; and she kept staying longer and longer. Old Annie and Jim didn't understand where little Maggie was going, and why she stayed away so long, and she didn't tell them.

She had a gold ring set with jade now, which she hid under her pillow so that Annie and Jim wouldn't see it. Then she started to stay away nights, and finally they only saw her once in a while. The last time she came she wore a queer looking blue dress with fancy em-

Tong Sing Wo

broidery all over the top, and under it there were pants legs hanging down. Her hair was cut straight across her forehead, and she had some flat green pieces set in gold strung around her neck; and now she let them see the jade ring on her finger. She didn't even look like their little Maggie, and, when she had gone, old Annie and Jim cried.

They moved their campody away over on the other side of town, where some other Indians lived, near the spring at the foot of Peppermint Hill, but they always were thinking about the little Maggie they had lost.

In the "Tong Sing Wo General Merchandise Establishment—Domestic & Imported," there were three floors. The first floor, filled with all the goods as listed on the sign, was about as far as most people ever got, or ever expected to get. Dark tales had come floating out as to what went on in those two upper floors, but that was the Chinks' own business, especially when that Chink happened to be Tong Sing Wo.

Little Maggie was frightened at first by what *she* saw on the second floor: dim lights, strange dark faces, gambling tables all through the place—lots of them, filled with players of fan-tan, faro, and other Chinese games. Most of the players were Chinks, but here and there was the face of a white man, or a white woman, strange and pallid. On the sides of the walls were the opium bunks, never empty. No one paid much attention to them, excepting those who were waiting for someone to vacate. There you could see the addicts in the different stages—from those who were twirling the little round ball in the flame of the lamp, before putting it in the pipe, to those who had done their smoking and were having heavenly dreams.

Chinatown vacated

The third floor was just an opium den, but it was on a grand scale. Teakwood bunks all closed in by silk curtains, if you wanted to pull them across. Only certain people, who were particular about their habits not being known, and who could pay for it, got in there. It was said, too, the opium was of a better quality.

The folks who frequented these places weren't long in finding out about Pretty Maggie, and they got used to seeing her parading around here and there in her Chinese finery. The pity of it was, she spent more and more time twirling that little wad around the flame, and lying in the bunk with the yellow curtains, that was reserved for her.

Things went on in this sort of way for a long, long time; then there were fewer players and the Chinks who did come didn't seem to be so interested in the games any more. They was a talking and chattering in their own native tongue, and Maggie didn't understand them. Then one day there was a hammering all around the place, and when Maggie went downstairs, in a drowsy sort of way, she came to the realization that the place was getting dark. Yes, there was no mistaking it, the windows were being boarded up.

Next morning there was a strange silence. Maggie had used more opium than usual the night before and was asleep late. When she finally walked out of the living quarters in the back there wasn't another soul in the building, and it was so dark she couldn't even see around. There was no fire and it was cold. It took some time for the truth to sink into her benumbed brain. Yes, Tong Sing Wo was gone, and with him his following of Chinese. Vaguely, Maggie remembered of hearing once about his wife and children in China, but what did it matter then—China was so far away.

There was plenty of food, nothing had been taken out, and there was opium, too, in the place where it was usually kept. She took little of the food and more of the drug. Days dragged on into weeks—and months, and she just wandered around, in an aimless way, like a creature that seemed to be more dead than alive. Then, with a start, she realized she was opening the last tin of opium. When that was gone her misery reached its height.

People passing heard a sort of wailing and moaning in the big empty place with the boarded windows, and they talked about the demented Indian girl who was inside. Then one night the door opened, and a pathetic figure ran from the dark house out into the moonlight. It sort of groped its way to the spot where Annie and Jim's campody used to stand. There was nothing there —only an empty lot. After resting for a while the figure

Annie and Jim (Annie face down crying)

moved over the ridge and across to the spring at Peppermint Hill.

Annie and Jim were asleep, but they awakened to hear a sort of cry and moan, and, crouching down in the corner on a rabbit skin blanket was the pathetic form of what had been their pretty little Maggie. She didn't speak then, or later, but they grew used to her silence and let her alone.

"China man's loco weed, heap bad," said the Indians.

Maggie used to roam around the hills, head down, always a looking at the earth. One day she came upon some plants that were just showing their heads above the ground. She pounced down on them, pulled them up by the roots and smelled them. Yes! These were what she had been looking for. She ate the roots, whole handfuls of them, the deadly poison parsnip.

Annie and Jim found her in a heap, stone dead, and as they lifted her to carry her home a gold ring set with jade slipped from her finger.

CHAPTER SEVENTEEN

Jim Pender Goes with Strangers on Tour of the Camp Today Telling the Story of Hank Blanchard and Others

Know what I'd like to do, pardner, that is if you and your friends don't mind. I'd like you to take me down the canyon 'bout three miles to the old stone Toll House. Seems as like I could get more into the spirit of my story if I could read that old sign once again. Thank you, Mister; glad you'd like to go. How about puttin' another bottle into your rig an' taking it along, case I get thirsty and couldn't go on with the story.

To the right are the Bodie dumps we're a passin', now I can remember the time when those old dumps were so covered with red calico you couldn't even see th' dirt. I don't blame you for smilin', Misses, seems like I *am* goin' crazy in my talk, but it was this-a-way.

So much good highgrade was thrown over with the waste in those there dumps that the squaws in the camp got wise about pannin' 'em and sellin' the gold dust to old Soderling, the assayer. Now a squaw, in those days, wouldn't wear anything but a red calico dress. Lordy God, no. You never seed a squaw that wasn't all togged out in red calico. When the ditch started runnin' in th' spring the mehalas all quit their washin' for the white woman an' they started washing dirt for themselves. They settled like a swarm of ants on those dumps a lookin' for the good pieces of rock, an' they knew 'em, too. The squaws had an eye for gold. They pounded the pieces of rock up in a mortar at the foot of the dumps and panned 'em out in the stream. Sometimes there was plenty of ice and snow along the stream, too, but th' red skins didn't mind. It was more to their likin' than

Dumps on left side, Milk Ranch Canyon in foreground

standin' over a wash board with th' hot suds comin' up in their faces, a tryin' to wash out dirt that had no gold in it.

A smart Indian, named Harry, built an arrastra, and run it by a mule goin' around. He would buy the pieces of rock from the squaws, an' the gold dust, too, but they preferred to sell it to old Soderling, the assayer, who had th' name of throwin' in a little "fire water" with the deal; an' that led to some killin' among the Indians, too.

See that house to the left up on the hill? Well, that's where Emma Goldsmith of The Ozark boarded out her little boy with a family named Stewart. Paid them handsomely for doin' it. 'Twas said she supported the whole family. When the little boy was ready to go to school Emma had them move away with the child, 'cause she wouldn't take a chance on some other kid tellin' her little boy what his mother was. Nearly broke Emma's heart, and for a week she cried, The Ozark on Maiden Lane was in darkness.

House on left side of road

Up there is what we call Milk Ranch Canyon; ran first by a Dago named Moresi, and later by Patroli. The milk wagon came around, with the milk in gallon cans; the Dago would whistle, and the housewife would come out with a container. She bought whatever she needed, from a quart up to gallons.

Now we're passin' the old Syndicate Mine. See the brick mill over there on your right, Mister? In early days R. R. Colcord was the Superintendent of the Syndicate. He afterwards was Governor of Nevada. A lot of money came out of that old mine, but the more gold the more litigation and trouble. Finally it was managed by Warren Loose.

Warren got his name plastered all over the San Francisco papers, when he brought suit against Leland Stanford to recover a colt. Seems Loose sold a racin' mare to Stanford, not knowin' she was in foal, and when the colt was born Loose up and claimed it. He lost the suit.

Warren Loose house

Then a young, pretty red-headed stenographer, who sat behind a desk in the Palace Hotel, up an' married him, maybe thinkin' he was a millionaire. When they landed back in Bodie, Warren stopped in front of a little three-roomed house. ''What are we stoppin'

Warren Loose's grave

here for?" demanded the bride. "This is our new
home," said Warren, "and, furthermore, you get up at
6 o'clock in the morning and cook my breakfast, 'cause
I have to work." He didn't carry his bride across the
doorstep, maybe she preferred to go on her own power,
but she must have been pretty weak from th' shock.
When she entered she put her head down on the big
square piano Warren had been braggin' about, an'
which took up half the space in th' room, and had the
hell of a good cry. She stayed along about three months.
Then Warren took her to Reno, kissed her goodbye,
and promptly looked around for No. 2. (Just another
little nip, please, Mister; my whistle's gettin' dry.)

Warren kept up his pace for years, then finally he
began consultin' th' doctors. They all advised him to
have his teeth pulled; nearly every one in his head had
a gold crown. This Warren refused to do. The pisin
in his system finally got him, but before he died he
sparred around for a vantage spot to be buried. "I
want a spot," he told the fellers, "where my grave can
be seen by everybody comin' in or goin' out of Bodie."
Lordy God—he was buried on the very highest spot he
could find, on the peak of Foundry Hill, south of the
cemetery. He has a nice stone monument over his grave,
which you can see on the right as you go out of town.

Now we're roundin' the hill to the old Toll House.
See the remains of the stone buildin' an' the old sign
lyin' across th' road? Lordy God—seems as if old
Hank should be steppin' out to greet us. If he did
you'd think it was the ghost of old Abe Lincoln himself, he looked so much like 'im. He was as honest as
old Abe, too. Was a graduate of Harvard or Yale, or
some of those big highfalutin' colleges in the east.

BODIE AND STATE LINE TOLL ROAD

Franchise Granted February 14, 1881, for the Term of 50 Years

RATE OF TOLLS FIXED BY THE BOARD OF SUPERVISORS AT THEIR SESSION, JANUARY MEETING, 1901

RATES OF TOLL

Buggy and 1 Horse	50 cts
Buggy and 2 Horses	75 cts
Wagon and 2 Horses	75 cts
Each Additional Animal	25 cts
Saddle Animal	25 cts
Loose Stock	5 cts
Freight Teams, Light	Half Rates
Wood Teams	Half Rates

H. C. BLANCHARD

Toll road sign

Maybe he was too strong in his likes and dislikes, but
if you were his friend he'd go to hell and back for you.
He came of a good family in one of the New England
states. His nephew, Noyes Westcott, wrote David
Harum, and sent old Hank a copy, inscribed on the
front page, "To the original David Harum, my uncle,
Hank Blanchard." Signed, "Noyes Westcott."

Hank was married to a charmin' lady, an' they had
two sons—Leet and Van. They lived in a house opposite the Methodist Church, which is still a standin'.
Mrs. Blanchard was a belle on the Comstock in th'
boom days of Virginia City. One of her sisters had
married the millionaire Shaw of New York, an' the
other the millionaire Isaac Requa of Oakland.
'Twasn't any wonder she didn't want to keep stayin'
in a place like Bodie, 'specially when old Hank was
away so much. Well, she finally moved to San Francisco, an' Hank made livin' quarters for hisself at the
Toll House.

He had located the only lime deposit around this
country, and built a lime kiln about six miles from
Bodie. Lordy God! 'T was said he made thousands of
dollars a year from his sale of lime to the mills and
cyanides in Bodie; an' he gave it all away. Hank just
didn't give a damn for money.

He was a good drinker, an' a good story teller, and
had a great love for horses. He had the shelves of his
room filled with good books, and could quote from all
the sages and poets, but his own witty sayin's were most
appreciated by everybody.

One time he and Charlie Hays were lost in a snow-
storm, when comin' in by team from Lundy. "How's
your sense of direction?" said Hayes. "Oh, hell!

Charlie," replied Hank, "I'd get lost in a two compartment water closet."

Another time the hotel keeper spoke to Hank about makin' so much noise when he went to his room late at night. "Now, Mrs. Perry," said Hank, "if you can roll a barrel of whisky up stairs with less noise than I made, I'd like to see you do it."

One day I was a listenin' when old Hank was talkin' to the local banker 'bout his finances. "There's nothin' like lookin' ahead and providin' for the future," said Hank, "I just paid ten dollars for the second hand grave of that old Chink they dug up to send his bones back to China. Feel I'm goin' to need it some day, an' Lester Bell has made a solemn promise to see I'm put into it."

Old Hank had his moments of regret, too. One time, at bein' asked by a friend to make a New Year's resolution to give up drinkin', he meditated and replied,

Hank Blanchard's Toll House

"I have given up my home, my family, my money, my self-respect for drink—now why should I give up drink?"

At one time he had a lawsuit in Bridgeport, and not likin' the Judge's rulin' durin' the trial, he up and told the Judge to go to HELL. "Mr. Blanchard," said Judge Virden, "I hereby fine you $30.00 or 30 days in jail for contempt of court." "Go to HELL again," responded Hank. "$60.00 fine or 60 days in jail," said Judge Virden, getting red to the roots of his hair, and his long beard, too. "Go to HELL and be damned," hollered Hank. The Judge hesitated, and finally with a gulp in his throat, "$90.00 fine, or 90 days in jail." "Go to HELL, HELL, HELL," bellowed Hank. The Judge, seein' as how he would have Hank broke, or in jail for the rest of his life, said to Sheriff Cody, "Please escort Mr. Blanchard to jail, Sheriff. Case postponed until tomorrow." A tribute to Judge Virden's sense of justice was that the case was decided in Hank's favor.

Lordy God! What do you think? Through stubbornness, old Hank served out his 90-day sentence—every day of it. Bein' a friend of Sheriff Cody he ate all his meals at the family table. Even subscribed for the Youth's Companion for all the children in the family, and read to them every day. (The subscription was renewed each year while Hank lived.) The followin' Christmas the four Cody children each received a gold penknife, engraved on one side with the child's name, and on the other side, "From Uncle Hank—Cell 13."

He was a sworn woman hater, but always kept a hot brick in th' oven of his stove to warm the feet of any woman who rode through in th' winter time. If he was away, up town, he had a sign painted which read "TOLL

CHAP AT SUNDAY SCHOOL." He collected no toll at all from his friends, an' he had lots of 'em. He called the Toll House "Camp Honesty."

That reminds me of an altercation he had in the saloon once with Bodie's Bad Man, Pioche Kelley. Each covered the other with a pistol. Then up speaks old Hank, "Say, Pioche, it's just this way, if I kill you I'll have the thanks of the community. If you kill me, I have plenty of friends that will take care of you." No shootin' was done.

Hank died in San Francisco, and was cremated. It was told it was his wish that his ashes be brought back and deposited in them bluffs up there—back of the old Toll House. His family came the followin' spring an' made a trip down here. 'Tis supposed they placed old Hank's ashes where he wanted 'em.

"Hand the bottle over, please, Mister, while I turn my face to them bluffs up there. Here's to you, old Hank, the original David Harum."

Now let's turn around, Mister, no use goin' much farther. There's a ranch 'bout four miles down, but nobody lives there any more. A big family was raised on it. Their names were Gregory. They were a studious bunch, those boys an' girls. Girls all turned out to be school teachers. The boy, named Spence, is a licensed United States Government surveyor an' engineer. We may run into him when we get up town, as, through choice, he still lives here. Loves to talk to the tourists, too, 'bout the old days of th' camp.

Turn around right here, Mister, and we'll go back to town. This is the place old Hank dug out for just this purpose. Built a barn over there for his horses. Lordy God! He used to drive spankin' teams.

You wouldn't believe it now, folks, but the main street used to come way down here. It was two miles long, buildin's on both sides. McKenney's Business Directory of 1882, of the principal towns in California, Nevada, Utah, Wyoming, Colorado and Nebraska, gives a two column write-up on Bodie, sayin' it was one of the richest minin' districts in America. This is followed by the Bodie Business Directory—pages long. Reads as if you could buy anything in Bodie, from minin' picks to champagne; and, Lordy God — talk about the professional men, as well as the gamblers and saloon men that thronged in here.

Then along comes the big fire of July 25th, 1892, an' sweeps th' business district plumb off th' map, 'ceptin' the block around where the Miners' Union Hall now stands. Them are the old original buildin's around there. I can point 'em out to you when we get up town. Well, after this fire part of the main street was rebuilt. Then in 1932 along came another fire, an' swept the main street just about the same. Again the Miners' Union Hall survived, so did the two large brick buildin's, an' the land office buildin'. Neither one of them fires spread to the residential section.

Now we're passin' the squaw dumps again, at the left, on our way back. See the old residence here on our right? The Dolan family lived there, an' a fine old family they were. Furnished two good Sheriffs for our County—Jim, who was killed in the performance of his duty, and Bert, who was Sheriff for over 20 years. He still lives in Bridgeport. God bless him!

Just a little farther on, up here on the flat, was Pioche Kelley's house; that's gone now.

There's the place where old Buffalo Bill had his

shack that was blowed to pieces, when he got that well deserved blastin'.

Over on that grassy flat is the site of the old Red Light District. The sheeps graze there in summer now. The herder pitches his tent 'bout where the "May Time" used to stand. Next to that was the place where "Madame Moustache" lived. Boys dubbed her that, 'count of her aversion to fellers who had hair on their faces. 'Tis said she got so much in debt through gamblin' she finally shot herself.

Now let's sidetrack here to the right and go past the old jail buildin'. It never was much of a jail, as you see. 'Side from the iron bars in the windows, might be a miner's cabin. The real dangerous prisoners, if the "601" didn't tend to 'em, was whisked off to Bridgeport pretty pronto. Drunken Indians was thrown in there, too, to sober up. Another drink, please, Mister.

Bodie jail

When the law was passed that a jail had to be fire-proof, the Constable, Ed Gray, had to lay off work in the mine to watch it, case a prisoner might burn to death. Last man locked in there sawed his getaway through the roof.

Now we're comin' into the old China Town District,

Scene from Bodie Chinatown

biggest one in California, next to Sacramento. In 1880 there used to be thousands of those pig-tailed Chinks, with their funny little trot up an' down this street, and they lived in their squalid little houses.

Tong Sing Wo was the big boss. Owned a store three stories high.

Yonder lived a little Chink, who was dubbed "Chickie Chinaman." He peddled fruit and vegetables around town, carried 'em in baskets strung on a wooden neck yoke. Weighed 'em out on a wooden stick, with pans a hangin' to th' winds. No one knowed how he did it, but you got the right weight.

There was a crazy Chink, Hoolie Ma, an' all the children in th' camp were scared to death when they saw him a comin'. Lordy God—how they would run to hide. He had long white hair that fell half over his face, an' he was always a mumblin' to the Chinese Gods.

Then there was old Charlie Chinaman, who replaced the cane seats in chairs. Used to have a long pole with cleats stickin' out the sides where he hung chairs. Looked like the Hangin' Tower of Pisa comin' toward you.

The laundry Chinks were a runnin' up and down with bundles of clothes on their backs, an' people was a dodgin' to get out of their way. Lordy God—I don't even have to shut my eyes to see that procession filin' past us now. It seems so real to me I can even smell the fumes of opium an' China whisky in the air. Let's get up the street again. This China Town is sort o' on my nerves.

Now we are back to our startin' point. Let's end up by takin' another drink. Thanks! You can put me off where you found me, in front of this old deserted buildin'. 'Course, as long as you *ask,* Miss, I do know a lot more stories, but don't feel up to tellin' any more today. You say you'll come back tomorrow, just to hear me talk? Thank you, folks. I'll be here to meet you. Lordy God—don't understand how you city folks could enjoy hearin' an' old wreck like me speelin' out these stories of the past.

CHAPTER EIGHTEEN

Jim Pender Resumes his Stories to Tourists next Day

Well, howdy, folks—thought some way you'd change your minds overnight an' not come back to listen to an old fool prattlin' an' goin' on about days that are dead an' gone in this old camp. Funny, though, how the memory of them lives on and sort o' haunts a person. Even in the night I'm dreamin' of those wild, excitin' days, an' if I wake up an' the wind is comin' through the windows where the panes of glass are broken out an' the moonlight castin' shadows on the wall, seem as if I see forms some way a flittin' here an' there. 'Course it's just my 'magination. Person gets that way bein' alone so much. Let's sit here in th' sun awhile this mornin', afore we start ridin' around again, an' I'll tell you some amusin' little stories.

Thanks, Mister, for the eye-opener.

There's been some pretty smart animals in this town. 'Twouldn't do to forget them in my stories of Bodie. Had the smartest mules here of any place on earth.

First one was a mule named Tom. Now Tom was about the biggest old brown mule that could be found anywhere. That mule knew his 'rithmetic without even havin' a teacher. His job was to pull the cars full of ore from the shaft level to an incline slope at the Standard Mill, an' he didn't even have to have a driver. There old Tom got free of the cars and they were toted to the top of the mill by a cable. Six cars was the load old Tom could pull easily, and as each car was coupled behind the other there was a loud click. That old animal would stand with his ears back awaitin' for that sixth click. When he heard it he was ready to start off, but if he heard a seventh click he wouldn't move a muscle. No, sir'ee, they could even whip old Tom an' he would just stand; but let 'em go an' uncouple that extra car an' the old cuss would start off. One day the cable broke at the incline at the mill and the cars began tearin' down at the rate of a mile a minute. Tom was a standin' on th' track right in th' path of the cars. Realizin' this danger, he just stepped off to the side and let the cars go a whizzin' past him. When noon came, old Tom knew it an' he would start off to the barn on the run. They tested out these things enough to know it to be a fact, old Tom could count an' he could tell time.

The white mule in the Standard Mine was another mule one heard a lot about. Lordy God, but miners are a superstitious bunch, always a tellin' tales as to how they have warnin's one way an' another.. I reckon 'twas about sixty years ago they decided a mule was needed to haul the cars on the 500-foot level in the mine. All the mules in the camp were too big to put into the cage to be lowered into the mine, so they bought a half-grown mule called Jerry at a ranch at Mono Lake. When Jerry was lowered into that

mine the miners knew he would never again see the
light of day. He'd grow too big to ever be taken out.
They built him a stall in a tunnel off to the side, an'
at regular times they took hay and water down to him
on the cage. Jerry did grow big, an' he did a lot of
work haulin' cars—with never a pay day. A mule
was needed on the 600-foot level after awhile, an' as
Jerry was too big to be taken up an' down on the cage
they built an incline connectin' the two levels so as
he could walk up an' down as he was needed. They
called this incline Mule Canyon. Then one day there
was a fire in th' shaft. All the miners were able to get
out, but, of course, poor old Jerry was doomed. When
that smoke poured in where he was, he suffocated. They
found him dead in his stall, just as they 'spected he'd
be, an' they dug a hole and buried him at the bottom
of Mule Canyon.

Once a miner told of seein' a white mule in the mine,
and when he was killed th' next day, Lordy God, how
the story spread. The miners got to joshin' each other
'bout seein' the white mule, but, just th' same, they
was all a little afraid they might.

The story is told that there was a certain man in town
who was so lazy that he wouldn't get out of his own
tracks. His wife had threatened to leave him if he
didn't go to work. He got a job in th' mine an' asked
the boss to put him on the 500 level. That night the
good-for-nothin' old cuss came home with the story
that he was diggin' a hole and as he was lookin' down
in it, just afore comin' off shift, he saw a little white
mule in the bottom. Lordy God, his wife started to
cry an' wouldn't let 'im go back to work again. 'Course
nobody believed it much, only his poor wife, but from

then on if any fellow stayed off work the miners would ask him, "What's the matter, did you see the white mule in the Standard Mine?"

JEROME AND MARGARET

The sign read "J. N. SALESBURY, CLOTHING, BOOTS & SHOES."

Now "Old Sal," as they called him, was subject to epileptic fits. He generally arranged it so as to have his fits at home. Then his wife, Margaret, could take care of him, and not do too much advertisin' about what was the matter with Jerome. One mornin', though, he sort o' miscalculated, an' fell in front of his store—frothin' at the mouth. Margaret was sent for in haste. She ran down th' street, an' when she reached old Sal she gave him two hard kicks, with the warnin' —"Get up, Jerome, you'll spoil th' business."

LOCAL TALENT

There was some good local talent here in the '80's; used to give a show often in the Miners' Union Hall. John F. McDonell would have made a good Shakespearean actor. He could quote old Shakespeare by the yard.

Florence Molinelli had a fine voice; afterwards made a name for herself on the legitimate stage.

Then there was a young fellow called Jack Dolan. He was an out-an'-out comedian. Jack surely missed his callin' by not gettin' into a minstrel show. One night Jack put up a job on a bashful fellow named Steve O'Brien. Steve was shinin' up to a local girl. Jack thought Steve would bring her to the show that night, so he had two seats saved for 'em in the front row. Sure enough, here comes bashful Steve and his girl. The usher toted them right up in front. Durin' the course of the performance Jack suddenly stopped in th' middle of his line. He was starin' straight at Steve an' his girl, his eyes and mouth both wide open, then he hollered out: "Oh! Steve O'Brien, let go of her leg."

COURT CASE

Back of the Catholic Church on Wood Street were two adjoinin' houses. A Scotch couple named Boland lived in one, and in the other was a couple named Hammer. Now, ol' man Hammer took to makin' coffins in his back yard, an' he used to be a slippin' in an' out of 'em to see if they was the right shape to be comfortable. Lordy God—he made one for himself, an' one for Barbara, his wife, durin' his spare time, an' stored 'em in the woodshed.

Barbara looked like a big, overgrown potato with eyes near the top.

It wasn't long afore the Bolands an' the Hammers were a fightin' like th' Kilkenny cats. Then old John Boland built a high board fence atween th' two houses. Lordy God—Barbara couldn't stand not to know what was a goin' on over at Bolands—so she poked out a knot in the fence so as she could peek through th' hole. 'Twasn't long afore old John got onto her peekin', so one day he sneaked along th' fence and dropped a big rock on Barbara's head. She lost no time in gettin' down town and havin' him arrested.

The case came up in the Justice Court. Neither of 'em hired a lawyer, preferrin' to plead their own cases. "Do you plead guilty or not guilty to the charge against you, Mr. Boland?" asked the Judge. "Not guilty," said old John. "Not guilty!" screamed Barbara. "Then will you tell me where in hell I got this bump on my head?" "Case dismissed," said the Judge.

Now, folks, let's start in where we left off yesterday on our tour.

*   *   *   *   *

So that vault that's standin' like a sentinel over there? That's all that's left of the Bodie Bank. Old

"All that's left of the Bodie Bank"

J. S. Cain opening safe whose contents had not burned

J. S. didn't think it was a goin' to burn, 'cause it escaped the fire of '92. Even when his granddaughters, Helen an' Ruth, went to him where he was directin' the fire fighters, an' asked him for the key to the bank so as they could save some things, he told 'em there wasn't any danger and said, with a smile, "You can save the chairs, anyway." Helen an' Ruth had been a helpin' all the folks along Main Street to save their belongin's. They went and opened th' Bank an' took the gold specimens and other things from the cabinet an' carried them across the street, in buckets, to what they thought was a safe place. They did save the chairs— 'bout the only things that were saved out of that old bank. "Wasn't any danger," Lordy God—in less than fifteen minutes the top of th' buildin' was burnin'. Some fellows ran to save the walnut counter an' it got lodged in th' door, an' that stopped everything. Helen an' Ruth an' their grandfather stood across th' street an' watched it burn. Helen was a holdin' a cabinet

Pat Reddy's cottage

specimen of the skeleton of a horned toad in her hand,
'cause it had seemed too fragile to be put in with th'
rocks, an' Ruth was a clutchin' a Websters Dictionary.

Next day when they went to get the specimens they
was gone; probably ground up for th' gold that was
in 'em. But the contents of the safe had not burned.

Up here a little farther was the General Merchandise
Store of S. B. Burkham, who had been prominent in
Lundy before comin' to Bodie. He an' his son, Cecil,
were partners. They had the stage contracts, too, runnin' th' stage lines to Hawthorne. Those were th' days
when the Wells Fargo messengers were still makin'
regular trips on these stages. Cecil married Josie

Last post office

Sieler, and is now in Nevada, a prominent rancher and business man of Reno.

Up that side street there is the little cottage where Pat Reddy, the great criminal lawyer, lived. Lordy God! but he was a fighter. Good thing, though, 'cause if he hadn't got his right arm shot off in a gamblin' row he probably never would have found he had such brains.

See that buildin' with th' sign POST OFFICE on it? Last post office Bodie ever had. Mrs. Mary A. McDonell was the last postmistress, raised a large family and spent most of her life here; an' that old buildin' has a history. It was the H. C. Osborne home in early days. He ran th' local paper. After th' fire of '92 it was moved from th' back street onto Main Street. Then when Eli Johl up an' married Lottie, of th' night life,

Land Office Building

he bought that house. Lordy God—he furnished it up
in style, too. It stood on th' other side of th' street,
near his butcher shop, but later it was moved over here.

Let's take a ride up Green Street now an' take a look
at th' schoolhouse. There it is with th' belfry on th'
top. It was originally th' Bon Ton Lodging House, run
in '79 by a Mrs. C. A. Ratjohn. Th' first schoolhouse was
two blocks up th' street, but a tough who didn't want
to go to school set fire to it an' burned it down. When
th' school was located in this buildin' the toughs sure
'nuf did get the upper hand. Lordy God, how they did
abuse the teacher. An old schoolmaster named Cook
even took a pullin' of his beard in a hand-to-hand encounter. That school was a battlin' ground. When
winter came they took to snowballin' the old fellow,
with hard-soaked snowballs, so he was afeared to go an'
come, and when the snow was gone they took to usin'
rocks. He did stay with it, though—'till th' term was up.

School house; dog sled in winter

Th' trustees advertised for a teacher for the next term, "big enough and brave enough to cope with the situation," for some of them kids in the seventh an' eighth grades was seventeen an' eighteen years old. Anyway, a man named McCarty applied; an' promised to run that school if he had to do it with a six-shooter. Well, he didn't exactly have to use a six-shooter, but he did use a long-handled black iron stove poker. Didn't even take the trouble to see if it was hot, sometimes; but he sure did battle them toughs. One by one they quit school. Mrs. Hearne bought th' stage contract to Lundy for her son Johnny, who was one of th' disturbin' element; an' the Garcia's, Kindbootz an' others sought new fields. By th' end of th' term that school was runnin' normally.

Now let's turn back to Main Street.

That long buildin', with th' brick annex, is th' old original Land Office buildin', later 'twas th' store of Bryant an' West. The United States Government sent

Miners' Union Hall

out as their Land Office Agent, M. J. Cody. He hailed from Lake Geneva, Wisconsin and was afterwards Sheriff of Mono County.

Sorry, Mister, I've been talkin' a long while now; seems like I could stand another bracer.

That old Miners' Union Hall over there was built in 1878. Houses some relics of the camp; hearses, gamblin' tables, finery of Rosa May, an' paintin's done by Mrs. Donnelly and Lottie; might be worth your while to visit it.

The brick buildin' we're passin' now, on this corner, was the store of Harvey Boone; great horse fancier was Harvey. Owned the Boone Stable an' Livery Business, too.

That house with all th' glass in front is the old Cain home. 'Twas moved down from its original location farther up this street. Lordy God, you wouldn't be-

Home of J. S. Cain

lieve it, but one horse an' one man moved that big house
almost a quarter of a mile. An old fellow named Pat
Manning took a contract to do it. He put it on rollers,
an' the horse just paraded round and round a big spool
windin' a rope attached to th' house. Didn't even break
the brick chimney, or fireplace. Old J. S. said he hesitated 'bout payin' him, though, 'cause he failed to move
th' well.

'Tis said that a ghost of a woman who died in that
house keeps a comin' back. She was the wife of th' man
who built the house, Jessie McGath. A Japanese house
boy refused to sleep upstairs because a big woman with
a sunbonnet and wide skirts used to come an' walk
around his bed. Took himself off to sleep in th' shed
to get away from her. Lordy God! Forty years later
a young school boy, who had never heard the Jap's
story, came down one mornin' tellin' th' same thing.
Martin Gianettoni, the watchman, who lives in th'
house now, says he wouldn't mind seein' the lady; says
she might be good company durin' th' winter months
when he is snowed in. How about drinkin' to the old
lady, Mister? Thanks.

That's the Methodist Church further up, built by
subscription 'bout '79. Seen lots of human happiness
and human misery, has that old church: weddin's,
social gatherin's, prayer meetin's, Sunday Schools, and
funerals. It's fallen pretty much to ruin now. E. J.
Clinton, of the Clinton Cafeteria in San Francisco,
spent a lot of money restorin' it in 1928. Fine man,
Mr. Clinton, as good a Christian as ever lived. Not
many years ago some young girls got a tin can and
nailed it on the door of the church with a notice over
it sayin' "HELP THE POOR GIRLS OF BODIE." The tour-

ists goin' in and out of the church read it—and quite a
lot of coins were left for the "POOR GIRLS." The boys
soon got wise, and, rubbin' out the word girls, put boys
in the place. Next day when the girls went to do their
collectin' there was no money. When they discovered
the treachery that had been played on 'em there was
plenty of rock throwin'.

Let's step inside the Church and read the Ten Com-
mandments, which were so often broken but held in
respect by the righteous. Thank you, gentlemen, for
removin' your hats. No, missus, I won't go up to the
cemetery as it has too many memories and *I want to
sleep tonight*. I'll just sit here for a while and meditate
and maybe—pray. I sometimes do. The road past the
door leads up to the cemetery. Good-bye, folks, and
may God bless you.

Restored Methodist Church

CHAPTER NINETEEN

Conclusion

And so they still come to Bodie, people of another generation; not as gold seekers, not as settlers of a frontier mining camp, but as tourists interested in the history of the wild, romantic past of this old town.

They roam through the cemetery, peer into the deserted houses, and try to visualize the life that has been and is no more.

People who get a thrill out of standing on the spot where Pioche Kelley (Bodie's Bad Man) shot and killed Charlie Jardine, or seeing the place where the vigilantes strung up Joseph DeRoche.

People who turn and look back as they are leaving Bodie, with perhaps a feeling of reverence for the pioneers who lived and struggled and died in this remote and lawless mining camp "on top of the world."

People whose high powered cars will, in a few hours, take them back to the pulsating heart of a big city. A city, perhaps, that Bodie's gold has helped to build.

Methodist Church showing road leading to the cemetery

Index